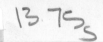

CULTURE OF THE SOCIAL SERVICES

Culture of the Social Services

ANDREW KAKABADSE
Cranfield School of Management

Gower

© Andrew Kakabadse 1982

Published by

Gower Publishing Company Limited,
Gower House, Croft Road, Aldershot, Hampshire, England

British Library Cataloguing in Publication Data

Kakabadse, Andrew
    Culture of the social services.
    1. Public welfare administration—Great Britain
    I. Title
    352.94'4'0491   HV248

    ISBN 0-566-00366-X

Reproduced from copy supplied
Printed and bound in Great Britain
by Billing and Sons Limited and Kemp Hall Bindery
Guildford, London, Oxford, Worcester

Contents

Contents

Tables

Figures

Acknowledgements

I would like to thank Richard Worrall for his assistance in both helping me develop ideas at the early stages of the project and for the collection and collation of the data. My gratitude to John Irwin of Gower Press for his invaluable advice on the direction the book should take.

Many thanks also to Iris White, Heidi Saunders, Sue Marriott and Sarah Bishton for their endless patience and perseverance in typing draft after draft in order to finally produce this document.

Finally, a special thank you to my wife for creating an environment conducive to the painful task of writing.

Introduction

This book is intended for social workers, senior social workers, residential officers and managers in the social services; in fact all practitioners in the field of social work. The book examines, through discussion and extensive research, the attitudes, beliefs, values and norms of work behaviour of personnel in social service departments (SSDs). The reason the thoughts, feelings and behaviour of personnel from all managerial levels in SSDs are examined, is simply that I consider it vital to understand the attitudes of persons who provide a personal service to members of the community. The basic product that any SSD offers is a service, through a human being (probably a social worker), to any member of the community. The effectiveness of that personal service is dependent on the attitudes, expectations, fears, disappointments and general personal competence, of the social worker, or in fact anyone who provides a personal service. Consequently, the attitudes that social workers, their colleagues and superiors develop towards their work, the department that employs them, the clients they service and the challenges of the future, are important areas of study. In fact, I argue that until one understands the attitudes and norms of behaviour that have developed in SSD's, all other studies on the provision of services to the community and the allocation of manpower within SSD's, are reduced to a level of unimportance. The reason for my somewhat 'wild' statement is that I consider the true determinants of people's behaviour at work to stem from the unwritten (at times unspoken) norms and practices that go on in every organisation. Fundamentally, organisations are powerful determinants of people's attitudes to work and their behaviour at work.

It is impossible to evade the influence of organisations on individuals, for two reasons:

1 *We live in a world of organisations*

Aside from certain artistic, craft or professional practises, virtually all work is done through human organisations. Even those who undertake quite singular artistic or professional activities cannot escape organisations. Apart from co-ordinating and providing a skilled service for those in large organisations, more often than not the craftsman and the lone professional is sponsored, either financially or in terms of having work referred to him, by the all pervading organisation.

2 *Organisations are a dominant influence on individuals*

Most people are aware to some degree, that the organisation they work for influences their attitude towards work, other people and the organisation itself. For example, most of us will have seen an individual, call him A, for whom it is far more important to show his superior that he can provide competent work and is worth considering for promotion, than it is to show his colleagues that he is a pleasant person who can work well in a team. Individual A is responding more positively to the influence of the hierarchy and authority than to his peer group. Individual B however, may hold colleague relationships in far greater esteem and hence, find individual A difficult to understand. Possibly, he may make no attempts to understand A and even speak of him in derogatory terms. For all of us who work in organisations, it is a common experience to have to come to terms with people who hold different expectations and beliefs to our own.

Both factors apply to SSDs. Social work is conducted in large organisations; in other words, departments that employ more than 800 persons. Most people who work in a large organisation will be influenced by the organisation. Some will agree and others disagree about what is done and the way it is done. For example, how should particular clients be handled; to whom should money be allocated; what services should be given priority and what should be the aims, objectives and purpose of the SSD in the community? These are differences of opinion on *what* should be done. Equally, there exists differences of opinion on *how* it should be done. People will hold different views on how work should be allocated within teams; to what degree should a supervisor control the activities of others; who should participate in what decisions and to what extent is it possible to appeal against and have revoked, unfavourable decisions?

The larger an organisation becomes, the more people debate what should be done and how it should be done. Why? First, there are more people in the organisation who have to make a decision and then live by that decision. Second, the larger the organisation, the more the resources available for distribution, which make the range of decisions that can be made, far greater. It is no surprise to see in any organisation disagreements and conflict as a part of normal everyday practise.

A decade has passed since social services in Great Britain were re-organised in 1970. The details of the national re-organisation are examined in Chapter 2. Suffice it to say at this stage that re-organisation created one organisation (the SSD) to provide for a unified social welfare service to the community, previously managed by the three separate local authority departments of children's, welfare and health. With such organisational changes, what has happened over this last ten years? What new areas of knowledge and practise have developed? Open most books or journals on social work and you will find that most of the texts concentrate on:

a) identifying new needs in the community;
b) identifying services to meet the new needs;
c) identifying new social work techniques and methodologies;
d) refuting outworn techniques and methodologies;
e) identifying current services that do not quite meet community needs and hence require attention.

In other words, issues of *what* should be done and the process of *how* it should be done, have concentrated virtually entirely on the practice of social work in the community. Other than one or two isolated pieces of work, the influence of the organisation on individuals and the practise of social work, has not been explored.

The emphasis of this book is on examining the 'what and how' of managerial and organisational practise in SSDs, and not on social work itself. A great deal of attention has been given to the provision of services to meet existing and new community needs, but little work has been done on what it means to be a field worker, supervisor or manager in an SSD. Just how important is it to be able to manage oneself, one's subordinates, one's colleagues and the total organisation? In fact, what does management mean in SSD's? Perhaps, reasons as to why these questions need answering can be provided by the two cases studied below.

Case A: recruiting a social worker

During the summer of 1973, I was involved in a research/consultancy project in an SSD in Scotland. My task was to help the department prepare itself for the traumas of local government re-organisation which was to follow one year hence. The role I played was that of an organisational analyst, i.e. a consultant or catalyst, helping people at various levels in the departmental hierarchy to think through, or even face, work problems that they could not face or manage on their own.

One afternoon, quite unexpectedly, a well respected senior social worker in the department burst into my office and stated, 'Well, what do you think of that?' 'That', turned out to be an application form sent by a social worker (an American) employed in a London borough SSD, in response to an advert for a vacancy that existed in the senior officers' team. I examined the form and concluded that the applicant was a well qualified and highly experienced social worker.

> 'Interview him as quickly as possible, before someone else offers him a job', was my response.
> 'What a person like that! You must be joking!'

I could not understand the response of the senior officer, nor for some time, the conversation that followed. His view was that the applicant was a 'charlatan', attempting to obtain employment under 'false' pretences. Further, the opinions of other colleagues in the department were similar to those of the senior social worker. The discussion was terminated abruptly by the senior social worker stating that I was ill-suited to my present position, 'if I could not see such a simple point as that'.

What was so simple and what was the point? Why the aggressive stance and language if a decision had already been reached on the non-suitability of the applicant? My opinion in that situation counted for little. Perhaps worse still, I may have lost credibility in that person's eyes and for a consultant to lose credibility in the eyes of the client, is a definite sign of failure.

However, the conversation was interesting for it indicated the criteria the senior officer used for reaching a decision about the situation.

1 The criteria the senior officer used to reach a decision were not explicit but assumed. Unless one knew the individual, it would be impossible to know the way he felt and thought.
2 The senior officer had not fully considered the merits of the applicant but had in mind a type of person he wished to appoint.
3 The criteria for appointment seem to have been commonly held by other members of the team.
4 The influence of the senior officer on other members was noticeable.
5 The senior officer's conversation with me indicated he was searching for confirmation rather than exploration of his point of view.

Case A is true, a little unusual but does help to provide answers for all of us who did not get the job we should have got. One man seemed to influence the attitudes of others to the point where only mediocre candidates were considered suitable for vacant positions. If this was the way he treated new appointees how exactly did he develop his team members; what did he consider as good supervision; and perhaps most important, what attitudes did he hold towards the various client groups with whom he came into contact?

Case B: the directors' seminar

I recently held a seminar for the director, assistant and divisional directors and principal officers in one SSD. The seminar was entitled 'Managing the Social Services'. During the meeting one director, frustrated by the discussions, demanded why his colleagues were viewing departmental affairs so simply. In his opinion, running an organisation did not just involve drafting and re-drafting organisation structure charts, attending meetings and supervising the work of others, but it involved obtaining a 'feeling' or 'sensitivity' about the organisation which helped put these activities into perspective. Further another aspect of managerial work, planning for the future, should not just involve extrapolating from present trends, but thinking creatively i.e. re-examining present practises in order to identify new activities for the future. He was greeted by howls of derision from his colleagues, but as the seminar progressed, no other participant offered more insightful comments.

It became apparent at the seminar, that the assistant and divisional directors did not fully understand why splits and conflicts occurred in their department, how people at the lower end of the organisation could become job dissatisfied and what it meant, in practice, to try and motivate other people.

After much debate, the participants at the seminar agreed on the following points:

1 Working in an organisation involves an individual holding membership with one or more groups within the organisation.
2 Working with a group of people does have a profound effect on an individual's beliefs, attitudes and behaviours.
3 In order to function effectively in groups, the ability to communicate with different people is vital.
4 Ineffective communication in groups and between groups is the norm in most organisations.
5 Understanding the reactions and behaviours of others does lead to improved communication.
6 New ideas and developments take time as people have to both understand and accept the proposals.

7 Planning for the future involves re-examining and not extra-polating from, present practise.

Cases A and B highlight some of the issues pertinent to people who work in large organisations, which SSDs have now become. For example, to what extent do individuals in positions of authority influence the attitudes, expectations and behaviour of others? Further, will that influence have positive or detrimental effects on the way work is done? It is true to state that senior managers may not be able to fully comprehend the reasons for the different beliefs, expectations and behaviour of personnel in their department as the organisations they manage are large. Consequently, managers and field workers need to be able to accurately express the reasons for the behaviours and attitudes of subordinates, groups of people, colleagues and work practises, to people with whom they have no intimate connection. There is a need for a language, so that people who have no personal knowledge of each other can converse accurately.

Need for a language

Any manager in an SSD needs to understand what is happening around him, why people are reacting to him the way they are and why he is finding it easy or difficult to do what he wants. In order to understand, a manager needs to be able to diagnose situations, analyse situations and provide prescriptions and recommendations on what to do in each situation. To adequately diagnose, analyse and prescribe, it is necessary to express oneself, and in order to be fluent in expression, one requires a language. In order to express social work theories and practises a complex language already exists. What does not exist within the social work field is a well understood language that represents managerial and organisational issues. My aim is to introduce such a language to those in social work organisations.

I identify one area for discussion; that of organisation culture. Culture is a nebulous concept for it refers to the personal values and beliefs that people in teams, groups and organisations seem to share. There exist norms that people establish in order to differentiate between acceptable and unacceptable behaviour. These norms are strongly influenced by the size of the organisation, the structural arrangements of the organisation and the styles and personalities of group leaders and group members. The size and structure of organisation and leadership styles determine the deeply held beliefs with which people identify and which in turn influence the inter and intra group relations. I hypothesise that whatever work is done and the way it is done, is determined by the cultural norms that exist.

Plan of the book

The book is split into two parts. Part I explores the concept of organisation culture; first in broad terms, then more specifically in terms of research studies on the organisation culture of the social services. Chapter 1 examines the concept of culture and the factors that are likely to influence major cultural changes in any organisation. In chapter 2, a hypothesis is offered; namely, the Seebohm (1968) proposals that stimulated social services re-organisation in 1970 in Great Britain, have led to a rise in bureaucracy in SSDs.

Chapter 3 concentrates entirely on describing the studies that I and colleagues have conducted in the social services over the past five years. The research programme has involved over 800 respondents and 12 SSDs. The ideas examined in chapters 1 and 2 are applied (in research terms) in chapter 3. The original studies were heavily statistically oriented. Although some statistics are used especially in the second to fourth sections of chapter 3 (pp. 57–105), most of the original tables have been substituted by diagrams. Probably most readers will find the discussion in the 'Mix of cultures' section most relevant, for there I provide my interpretation of the types of organisation culture in SSDs.

Based on the results of the studies in chapter 3, recommendations for future practise are made in Part II. The recommendations are divided into two; issues concerning the organisational design of SSDs, and ways of improving the process of integrating individuals with their department. The reason that both design and person-to-person management type recommendations are made, is that SSDs are considered similar, in some of the problems they face, to other large organisations. Managing conflict constructively, motivating employees and improving the levels of service to the community may involve a single manager improving the relationship with his team, or it may equally involve re-examining the present structure of the department. Whether to apply person-to-person management practises or whether to enter into areas of organisational design and strategy, depends on the point of view and commitment to change of each individual, whether he be a fieldworker or manager. My aim is to present problems I have identified through research, offer possible alternative solutions, and thereby stimulate a debate amongst superiors, subordinates and peers so that the points of view of the major interest groups in SSDs will be appreciated.

I have tried to keep the number of references in the text to a minimum so that the busy practitioner can gather the threads of the arguments and see whether they apply to him. Should anyone wish to follow-up any references or studies, certain key texts are identified in each of the chapters. These are generally available.

Finally, why have I written this book? The answer is simple. The management of a large organisation (which I consider SSDs to be) is an equally important area of study as are studies of the services that the organisation provides. There exist few management type books for social services personnel and most of those are concerned with telling practitioners what they should be doing (see chapter 2). In contrast, I attempt to analyse what is currently happening and hence build recommendations around the results of the research studies rather than tell people what is the right and wrong way of managing their work affairs.

I am critical of some of the attitudes that I see developing amongst personnel in the social services. Why? Any situation in life is constantly in a state of flux and development. What happened yesterday, for example, social services re-organisation in 1970, has to be reconsidered today for the benefit of tomorrow. My feeling is that such reconsideration is not taking place within SSDs. Most certainly, people are attempting to identify immediate problems within their organisation and their work and are sincerely and strenuously attempting to put their situation right. What I do not see happening, is a re-examination of present practice in such a way that will help fieldwork practitioners and managers in SSDs understand why they are behaving and feeling the way they are and what should they do about it. Such a framework existed in 1970. A decade later, that framework needs re-examination.

As with every author, only some of the ideas presented are my own. Those that helped me develop specific ideas, I mention in the text. The numerous other discussions I have had with people sufficiently interested to talk to me in informal settings such as at the dinner table, at the bar or over a game of snooker, I am sorry. Although I have forgotten who you are, your basic ideas have stuck with me and have been used throughout this book. I only hope that I have used your thought provoking ideas in such a way that they will be of interest to others as they were to me.

A.P.K.
May, 1981

PART I

CULTURE OF SOCIAL SERVICE DEPARTMENTS (SSDs)

1 Culture of organisations

All of us recognise that cultural differences exist between people of different nationalities. From one country to another, people speak a different language, dress differently, enjoy different cuisines, and identify with different social customs. We also recognise that cultural differences exist within any one country. In England we talk of differences between a northerner and southerner and in fact, numerous jokes have emerged that highlight cultural differences and stereotypes.

In contrast, differences of culture are a more difficult concept to comprehend when applied to organisations. Yet, all of us have experienced cultural differences in organisations. When we change jobs from one organisation to another, we know that simply becoming acquainted with the technical aspects of the new position, will not be sufficient. If we are to be considered successful, we have to make a stringent effort to understand our new colleagues, superiors and subordinates and their attitudes towards work, supervision and the organisation in general. In our previous position, we may have been hardworking, conscientious and recognised by our colleagues as making a positive contribution. In the new job, to work too hard may be undesirable and to interact too closely with colleagues and superiors may be considered as 'social climbing'. After a time, all of us realise, that there are certain ways of doing things; there are certain subjects that are taboo, and there are certain people one can upset, but others one should never upset. In fact, all of us are surrounded by certain likes and dislikes which we must take into account in our daily work.

It is these likes and dislikes which are indicative of the attitudes which determine the behaviour of people in organisations. After a time, these attitudes and behaviours can become characteristics of a particular organisation. Various organisational characteristics such as leadership, supervisory styles, organisational structure and flow of communications, interact to produce something known as the *culture of an organisation.*

One thing is difficult to do, and that is define organisation culture. It is best described as a feeling which a number of people share consistently about certain situations. If a sufficient number of people perceive a situation in a similar light, does it then become reality? The answer is probably yes and if such thinking is applied to organisations, then a culture or a number of cultures may form amongst the various groups operating within the organisation. Handy (1976) goes further by indicating that cultures are a deeper phenomena than just a commonly agreed way of perceiving a situation amongst a group of people. Handy states:

> In organisations, there are deep-set beliefs about the way work should be organised, the way authority should be exercised, people rewarded, people controlled. What are the degrees of formalisation required? How much planning and how far ahead? What combination of obedience and initiative is looked for in subordinates? Do work hours matter, or dress, or personal eccentricities? . . . Do committees control an individual? Are there rules and procedures or only results? These are all parts of the culture of an organisation. (p. 177)

Culture can take on many meanings ranging from the types of buildings, offices or branches utilised to house the organisation's employees, to the kinds of people it employs, their particular career aspirations, their perceived status in society, their degree of mobility, level of education, and so the list continues. Hence, culture refers to the way people in different (or sometimes similar) work organisations view the world, their life and the way they go about their work. Even within one organisation different cultures will prevail; the different points of view that will exist between those working in research, the administration of residential establishments, policy making and field social work. Is it then possible to determine the different types of culture that exist?

Substantial research and discussion has centred on what are appropriate measures of the culture of organisations. A brief review of some of the possible measures will give an indication of the breath of scope.

Structure. This is an important dimension that crops up time and time again in the literature, usually as a subject in its own right. Structure has been taken to mean both structure of the organisation and structure

12

of the job. The structure of the organisation is often related to size. In most cases, the larger the organisation, the greater the distance from the top-level executives to the operating employees. This distance creates a psychological barrier in that those employees away from the decision making centres may perceive themselves as being out of the mainstream activities. Such a feeling of distance may generate a feeling of impersonality because of the difficulty to interact with others socially. Studies examining the degree of structure exercised over the job attempt to understand people's feelings concerning the constraints imposed by a superior or organisation upon an individual. Although structure is not considered to be a variable of culture, it is recognised as an important influence in determining the culture of an organisation.

Leadership patterns. There are a wide range of leadership styles that are utilised in companies, schools, hospitals, local and central government agencies. Leadership practises can be a major force in creating a culture which influences peoples satisfaction at work and the quality of their outputs.

Challenge and responsibility. This dimension examines peoples perceptions of challenge, demand for work and opportunity for a sense of achievement. The challenge aspect appears to be strongly and positively related to the development of achievement motivation among employees. In other words, it is presumed that achievement motivation is nurtured in a climate that allows employees a significant amount of responsibility.

Warmth, support and consideration. The key issue here is positive reinforcement rather than punishment for task performance. Positive reinforcement could mean an employee viewing that his superiors see him as a genuine human being. Equally, warmth and support could represent different kinds of work related anxieties. It is often assumed that employees who have institutionalised helping roles, such as doctors, nurses, social workers, have a strong affiliation need. In other words, what they desire is a warm and supportive work climate for themselves.

Reward and punishment; approval and disapproval. How effective are reward or punishment measures applied in a work situation? An assumption often made is that an environment oriented toward providing rewards, rather than metering out punishment, is more likely to arouse employee interests in achievement and affiliation and reduce a person's fear of failure.

Performance standards and expectations. Here the perceived import-

13

ance of performance and the clarity of expectations concerning performance that exist in the organisation, are measured. Achievement has been related to standards of excellence, and if the standards are high and people are given the opportunity to flourish, then achievement presumably leads to further achievement.

Conflict. This measures the perceived atmosphere that prevails among individuals and units within an organisation. It is a truism that organisations are continually faced with conflict minimisation and conflict resolution situations. Perhaps the resolution of conflict is one of the most important processes in the integration of organisational functions. It is important to note that the way conflict is resolved is as significant as resolving it. The manner of conflict resolution may be a strong predictor of the effectiveness of any attempts at integration of organisational functions.

Organisational identity. How loyal do employees perceive themselves to be and to whom is the loyalty directed — to the organisation as a whole, or to one's immediate group, or to certain individuals? A number of studies have found that emphasising group loyalty has led to increased group identity and improved performance.

These are some of the dimensions that have been identified and measured in industrial and public service organisations. Different organisations depending on their size, structure, geographic location, their product array, would behave differently on the above dimensions. However, each of the above dimensions would be interacting with each other and showing at different points, a strong or weak emphasis. In thinking about cultures and applying such thinking, one is attempting to construct a fairly comprehensive picture of the development of attitudes within any organisation.

The cultures

It is necessary to be able to analyse the position of the individual in certain situations; whether he is determining the situation for others, or being determined by it. A distinguished scholar and consultant, Dr Roger Harrison, has provided a means to help analyse the position of the individual in different cultures. Harrison (1972) identified the power, role, task and person cultures.

Power culture

A power culture is one that provides excitement and exhilaration for some and is substantially threatening to others, for this cultural type depends on strong leadership from a central power source (see Table 1.1). A central power figure or small group controls and manipulates all activity within the organisation. The power figures are usually accompanied by functional specialists who provide professional advice and information to further promote the image of the all powerful.

Traditionally, the type of organisation that has held such an image has been the small entrepreneurial organisation of the 19th Century. In the 20th Century, the industrial barons and some top, powerful trade union leaders have held an equivalent image. In addition, certain key executives in import/export companies, trading and finance companies may fall into this category.

Table 1.1

Power culture

Key dimensions	Key observable behaviours
Structure	Rules, regulations and procedures are likely to be in operation but unlikely to be adhered to by the key power figures.
Leadership	Strong, decisive, somewhat uncompromising; charismatic leader behaviour. Leader tends to manipulate others to satisfy own ends.
Challenge and responsibility	High risk taking and becomes involved in many situations. Key power figure responsible only for himself and possibly one or two staunch supporters.
Warmth and support	Low warmth and support for others by key power figures.
Reward and punishment	Mistakes and misdemeanours are punished if they threaten key power figures. Rewards are offered for pleasing or supporting key power figure.
Performance standards	Performance standards are not based on professional criteria but on maintaining influence over others.
Conflict	Key power figure operates in conflict situation by challenging others; vengeful if challenged by others.
Identity with organisation	Makes outward show of identifying with the organisation but inwardly is more concerned with his next job move.

A power culture oriented organisation functions mainly by subordinates anticipating the wishes, decisions and attitudes of those at the top. In practise, those at middle and lower levels will react quickly to rumour and use the grapevine as the main source of information.

15

Although regulations may be formally stipulated, in practise few rules and procedures are adhered to, as bureaucracy is viewed as more of a hinderance than help. In-fighting at the top of the organisation can be intense and a number of casualties may result both at the top and lower down the organisation. In a power culture, decisions are largely the outcome of a political struggle rather than logical deduction.

Such a culture can be summarised by words as competitive and challenging. The actors in the fray have to be seen as strong, proud and able to accept ever increasing responsibility. The power holders must be agile and flexible in order to react to danger and change course due to unpredicted influences in the external environment. Yet, whether the right or wrong decisions are made, the power holders paramount objective is their continued success and prosperity.

Persons who perform well in power cultures are not professionals in the traditional sense of presiding over an area of responsibility and valuing a limited amount of technical expertise. Professional activity is seen as constraining and de-motivating. In a power culture, money and status tend to be far more highly valued. Both money and status will be utilised to charm others so as to add to the powerful man's list of contacts. To this end, considerable time and effort is invested in creating and maintaining networks of potential sources of useful people, valuable information and keep an accurate diary of future events in order to extend their sources of influence.

Consequently, a power culture is one where personal success, charisma, intuition, constant change and risk-taking are virtually common, everyday experiences. A power oriented leader in a power culture, if successful is likely to be considered a source of inspiration. A power oriented leader operating in any of the other three cultures following is likely to be viewed with suspicion, mistrust and probably considered immoral.

Role culture

The role culture is one where functions, job specialisation, procedures and rules are seen to predominate. (see Table 1.2) Consequently, far greater attention is given to job descriptions, definitions of authority relationships, procedures for communication, rules for the settlement of disputes and an urgency to establish suitable cross-over points. The principal function of senior management is co-ordination, as once direction is given, each of the functions guided by rules and procedures will work according to the overall plan.

In a role culture, the formal definition of tasks and roles is considered more important than the individual. Individuals are selected to roles because the person is considered to fit into the role. It does not matter so much that one individual may be considered competent but

16

Table 1.2

Role culture

Key dimensions	Key observable behaviours
Structure	Well defined authority relationships; rules; procedures; detailed job descriptions.
Leadership	Leader power comes from the rightful issuing of rules, procedures and allocation of work.
Challenge and responsibility	To work within one's role and not threaten the existing role structure.
Warmth and support	Support offered in order to achieve the requirements of one's role.
Reward and punishment	Rewards offered for maintaining the existing role structure. Punishment given if too little or too much is done.
Performance standards	Measured by the requirements set for each role. Individual capacity is assessed only for purpose of attaining role requirements.
Conflict	Only when the existing rules, procedures and form of communications are threatened.
Identity with organisation	All organisational members are expected to identify with the organisation and work within the existing career structure.

more that he or she is capable of working within a particular role. Performance beyond the role is not required. Indeed, competent performance beyond role requirement can be seen as a threat by both colleagues and superiors.

Personal power is considered immoral in organisations that are role culture oriented, as power must be seen to emanate from the organisational role. Power here is acted upon in terms of the rightful issuing of rules and procedures and the appropriate allocation of work. Responsibility must be seen to be achieved on a rational basis. Such an organisation is synonymous with the sociologist Max Weber's, (Weber 1947) ideal bureaucratic form. The predominance of rules and procedures as a form of communication, the allocation of work to roles rather than individuals and the rationality of the hierarchy, are the principal features of Weber's rational-legal model.

A role culture organisation can only operate effectively in a stable social environment. Either, the external environment is unlikely to change, or the organisation has control of its environment through a monopoly. If one or both conditions are satisfied then, a role culture organisation may well be effective in its performance and output. The major national banks and insurance companies operate in stable, controllable markets and hence, are successful role cultures.

Yet, there exist organisations that have held a monopolistic position for a number of years, have developed stable, well established role cultures but suddenly face immense problems when certain product innovations destroy their monopolistic hold of the market. A current example would be in the telecommunications industry, where parts of the British Post Office have serviced not only the United Kingdom but installed communication systems in countries throughout the world. Innovations in America and Japan and the sudden popularity of micro-chip technology has thrown an immensely large organisation into a state of mild anxiety. The organisation no longer operates in a stable environment but now has to consider leadership issues in terms of selecting the right managers to manage in a crisis, product innovation issues, marketing issues and in fact develop into a matrix type organisation.[1] The alternative is to collapse.

For the social services, the Rowbottom-Kogan proposals discussed in the next chapter (chapter 2) closely resemble prescriptions for the creation of role culture organisations. The tasks allotted to each role and the emphasis on vertical differentiation are the striking features of the BIOSS unit's work.[2] For individual social workers employed in such a culture, security of job and predictability of career are important features of working life. Specialist expertise can be acquired with little risks and without too much haste. For individuals, there exists certain disadvantages. Those persons wishing to enter into new fields of endeavour and tackle completely new problem areas are unlikely to be successful in a role culture. Actions taken in a role culture are either approved or disapproved; rewarded or punished. Not surprisingly intuitive-innovative type people do not respond well to such stimulii.

It may be inevitable that role cultures will form in every growing organisation as economies of scale become more important consider-ations than flexibility. Managing a large number of personnel with varied technical expertise does demand clear cut role boundaries. The price to pay for the operation of such a system is loss of innovation and cost reduction.

Task culture

Task cultures attract persons whose preference is towards solving new problems. Groups of experts gather to focus on a common task or problem whether it be an organisational problem or one of a technical

1. For a discussion of matrices, see pp. 31-3.
2. Brunel University Institute of Organisation and Social Studies.

nature (Table 1.3). Charisma and influence are based on technical expertise rather than positional or personal power.

The predominant style is to work in team settings, rather than as individuals maintaining a role within the hierarchy or pursuing personal power needs. The task culture is a group culture, where differences of individual objectives, status and style are quickly sacrificed for the continued life of the team. Persons in task culture settings can quickly identify with the objectives of compact units (i.e. social work teams) but may have difficulty in respecting the overall objectives of their employing organisation.

Table 1.3

Task culture

Key dimensions	Key observable behaviours
Structure	Technical expertise is more important than Organisation Structure and Job Structure.
Leadership	Status and personal charisma based on knowledge and high technical performance.
Challenge and responsibility	Challenge is geared towards solving new problems. Responsibility towards members of the project group.
Warmth and support	High group support for project group members who display competence in technical skills.
Reward and punishment	Rewards for high task performance, such as project leadership or responsibility for solving bigger problems. Punishment for low task performance would be rejection from elite project team.
Performance standards	Based on problems at hand and technical expertise available. Standards do not always remain static but change according to the problems and personnel available.
Conflict	Can occur over differences of expert opinion. Such differences could lead to disbandment of the project group.
Identity with organisation	Identity centres on the project group. When group achieves its objective, members disband in search of new problems.

A major advantage of a task group is its adaptability. Project teams and task force groupings are relatively quickly formed to grapple with a problem area and are equally quickly abandoned on solution of the problem. Establishing formal roles has little meaning in such situations, as judgement is based on expertise, control over one's work, easy working relationships and mutual respect based on personal capacity. Hence, the task culture and the role culture are an anathema to each other. The former based on sensitivity and flexibility to the needs of the market and social environment, and the latter on the need to achieve somewhat inflexible but long-term objectives and establish rules, procedures, and roles for control purposes. The task culture thrives on speed of reaction, integrity, sensitivity, creativity as opposed to career hierarchies and role specialisation.

As control is not easy in task cultures, large organisations especially, face a number of problems. In organisations where a task culture predominates control remains in the hands of top management by means of allocation of projects, people and resources. The actual control of projects is left to project leaders or those occupying a supervisory position and hence, a decentralised task system but centralised policy system develops. When resources become scarce and project leaders have to justify their activities and ask for further resources, substantial negotiation and bargaining takes place. An immediate reaction by top management would be to control not only the allocation of resources but further daily task activities.

Such a move would be challenged by team leaders in an attempt to counteract the influence of senior management and thereby ensure that the team leaders will be competing with each other and not just with top management. In situations of no growth, allocation of resources to one area could mean a cut for another field of activity. From a positively oriented task culture where high personal expectations and performance standards are the norm, in periods of recession, morale in work groups could begin to decline. Job satisfaction will be reduced and the work group will disintegrate. Individuals will begin to pursue their own objectives. Management, in order to control the situation will introduce further rules and procedures and regulations and thereby begin to change a task culture into that of a role culture.

Organisations exist where the task cultures and role cultures exist side by side (see chapter 3). Such a phenomen arises when an organisation has experienced exceptionally rapid growth. General Electric Company (GEC) is a good example of a company that grew out of all recognition due to mergers and takeovers. The social services, local government and health services are similar, where national re-organisation changed the size and identity of the original organisations (see chapter 2). Fundamentally, the new public service organisations were conceived and planned in terms of role structures. Little emphasis during the period of re-organisation was placed on the task activities within the organisations. The resulting situation is that two, possibly incompatible, cultures exist within the same organisational setting. The directorate of the organisation is predominantly concerned with managing a role structure whilst the professionals and specialists favour smaller, informal work groups and task operations. In such circumstances, overall organisational identity is likely to be low. Task oriented specialists are likely to perceive management as being rigid and even manipulative and untrustworthy. On the other hand, group identity is likely to be high with substantial respect shown towards colleagues.

The task culture is one that the behavioural scientists of the 1960s and 1970s championed, placing emphasis on the advantages of small groups, expert power and the merging of individual and group objectives. The task culture has been held synonymous with change, adaptation, democratic freedom, choice and the reduction of differences of status. Yet in periods of economic recession, stringency or even rapid growth, it is doubtful whether such a culture would predominate. Most certainly, not all organisations are influenced by a task oriented culture and that is not because those organisations are immoral or out of date, but that such a culture is inappropriate to their technology, structure and resultant group norms.

Person oriented culture

The primary objective of the person oriented culture, is to serve the individuals in that group. Existing organisational structures, rules, procedures and roles are there to provide for the needs of individual members. (Table 1.4) The formal aspects of the organisation are prone to substantial change according to the needs and wishes of the actors in play at that moment in time. In practise, this is the rarest of the four cultures and Harrison has indicated tkat it is one that offers a higher order of moral values. For example, consideration of the other would take place amongst professional partners such as planners or architects, commune type environments, small consultancy outfits and possibly voluntary help task forces that provide assistance and friendship to individuals in need.

Control in such organisations can only function effectively by mutual consent. Each person has to have established with other group members a psychological contract (an understanding) that the individual is superior to the organisation. Ideally, each individual can leave the organisation when they wish and the organisation should not contain the power of eviction. In practise, a compromise position has to be reached.

Closed order of nuns. In a recent BBC programme entitled 'Decision', the personal traumas and doubts that a young woman faced just before entering a Closed Order of Nuns, were recorded. From the point of view of the nuns, they would not simply allow anyone into their Order. The first year was considered to be an apprenticeship experience and at the end of that time, not only was the individual free to leave but all

21

the nuns in that community voted as to whether the individual in question should stay. From there on the individual could leave or stay without any interference from the community. The evidence in the programme indicated that the nuns had established a person oriented culture by their concern for each colleague's welfare. The only control the organisation put into practise was at initial entry.

Table 1.4

Person culture

Key dimensions	Key observable behaviours
Structure	Changes according to the individuals in the situation. No long established rules and procedures.
Leadership	Principle of sharing and partnership predominates. All have equal say in the development of the group.
Challenge and responsibility	Each person is responsible for other group members. It is a challenge for each to help develop the support.
Warmth and support	Emphasis on personal growth by developing a warm and supportive environment.
Reward and punishment	Reward is being accepted by peers. Punishment is being asked to leave the group.
Performance standards	Jointly agreed by all members of the group. Individuals are expected to adhere to their standards.
Conflict	Conflict usually between cohesive group and larger organisation. If conflict occurs within the group, the group may disband.
Identity with organisation	Little allegiance to total organisation. Loyalty to the individuals with whom one interacts.

It is unlikely for a person oriented culture to predominate in an organisation that is medium sized and larger (i.e. over approximately 100 persons). In most organisations however, one is likely to find individuals and small groups whose preference is towards a person oriented approach but have to accommodate a stronger alternative culture. Some professional university staff for example, may hold strong person oriented values and task values but tend to operate in a role culture. Other than teaching and possibly some research, university staff tend to regard the organisation as a base from which to pursue personal professional interests, often which only indirectly add to the status of the organisation. The organisation however, operates according to quite a strict role distinction, especially between professorial and lecturing staff.

Other specialists in organisations often operate in a similar fashion; computer personnel, project engineers, hospital consultants and to an extent social workers. It is not unusual for people who hold these positions to feel little allegiance to the organisation but hold great loyalty to each other and to the client groups with whom they work. Once a satisfactory conclusion has been reached with one client group and new and pressing problems appear elsewhere, the person/task oriented professional will try to move to meet new needs. Such individuals will place high emphasis on personal warmth, support and consideration towards others.

As control depends on members' consent and co-operation, it is difficult to continue the development of a co-operative system over long periods of time. The founding member of a communal setting is likely to impose his own identity on the organisation. On his departure, the organisation will have to adjust either by developing into a different sort of culture, or by witnessing internal strife amongst potential leaders. By and large, an organisation that overcomes the difficulties of the leader's departure, changes from a person oriented culture to a task culture and sometimes to a role culture.

In the case of person oriented cultures which are a part of another but more dominant culture, control is always a problem. Managers within the organisation are likely to discover that specialists who are person oriented are difficult to manage. To direct their activities or influence their personal values would be virtually impossible as the normal range of sanctions brought to bear on erring individuals in organisations, would be meaningless to the specialist. To begin with, many specialists enjoy tenure of employment, but for those who do not, they at least will understand their position in the job market. For most specialists, their services are in demand and so to move is no real problem. Hiring outside experts is unlikely to alter their opinion and the power of a manager's personality is unlikely to impress the person oriented specialist.

Structure influences culture

Organisation structure is all-pervasive for anyone who has any contact with organisations. For a new employee, structure is an imposed condition as soon as he is told to report to his supervisor. In so called relatively loose structures, such as academic institutions, a structure exists based on publications, expertise and seniority. A customer or client dealing with an organisation similarly faces a structure when they select goods to buy or a service to meet their personal needs. They may be interviewed by one organisational member, referred to a second who it is thought can satisfy their needs better, and may be charged for the service by a third. Organisation structure is all embracing. In order to understand how influential cultures develop, it is necessary to scrutinise the underlying structural conditions.

Why analyse structure

John Child (1977) provides three reasons why the structure of organisations needs to be more closely analysed.

1 Organisation structure is necessary for the successful implementation of plans by providing a means whereby people and resources can be allocated to tasks that have to be done, and for identifying mechanisms that will allow for their co-ordination. This aspect of structure involves job descriptions, organisation charts, and the mechanisms of boards, committees and working parties.

2 People need some sort of indication of what is expected of them in their job. Where a task can be well defined, devices such as standing orders or operating manuals identify a step by step procedure for the completion of that task. Where a task does not easily lend itself to detailed definition, standards of performance can be established, incorporating criteria as output or quality of achievement. Some organisations would follow these up with an accompanying performance review of the individual in his job. Control procedures need not be the only way of forming job expectations, for other operating mechanisms, such as reward and appraisal systems, planning schedules and systems of communications, can be put into practise.

3 Within the framework of structure, provision is made for decision making and the dissemination of information. Arrangements have to be established for the relevant information to be collected from outside the organisation, partly by introducing specialist jobs for these duties. Not only collection, but the collation and evaluation of information has to be formalised whereby information can be made available to decision makers on a regular basis in response to new developments outside the organisation. The process of decision making can be assisted through programming, i.e. specifying key stages in the process and allowing for information to be fed back in order to review and re-appraise the original decision.

There is probably little to argue about in saying that the allocation of responsibilities, the grouping of responsibilities, decision making, co-ordination and control are all fundamental requirements for the continued operation of an organisation. What is hotly disputed is their combination, for there lies the basic quality of an organisation's structure which in turn effects the daily functioning and long-term development of the organisation.

Any change of structure will affect people's values, attitudes and work behaviour. If the changes of structure are slight, i.e. a simple re-location of the existing pattern of work, supervision, quality control procedures and existing resources, it is unlikely that any changes will occur in the basic cultural pattern. Even though an individual or group may gain or lose marginal resources, it is unlikely that there will be major changes in the commonly held attitudes prevalent in the organisation at the time.

Major changes in attitude occur when substantial changes of organisation structure take place. Such major changes of structure are usually referred to as *re-organisation*. As a result, re-organisation brings with it a number of problems. There exists three basic problems with re-organisation:

1 Key decision makers may simply be unaware that basic changes of structure may be accompanied by fundamental changes of attitudes and beliefs by most employees towards their work and employing organisation. Re-organising a total organisation may in the long run, create more problems than solve them. Deviations of some magnitude can occur between what is supposed to happen through re-organisation and what actually happens in terms of peoples attitudes and work behaviour.

2 Key decision makers may realise that changes of attitude amongst their personnel are required, but do not know how to develop these changes of attitude. Similar to the key decision makers in (1) above, they may attempt to change the structure in a specific attempt to change the attitudes of their personnel. Similarly, deviations of some magnitude are likely to occur between what is supposed to happen and what actually happens.

3 The vast majority of personnel in an organisation who have to respond to structural change may themselves be unaware that their own attitudes have changed towards their peers, superiors, subordinates, clients, work practise and hence, their attitudes towards their professional identity.

Consequently, it is important that when major structural changes are being planned that the relationship between structure and culture is understood. The key features of structure relevant to SSDs that will

25

seriously influence peoples attitudes and work behaviour are: size of organisation, complexity of relationships, and professional *v* organisational values.

Size of organisations

The size of SSDs is probably one of the most pertinent issues in social work today. The last decade has witnessed an extraordinary growth in the personal services from the three smaller units of children, welfare and mental health to the unified SSD. Yet, no more than six years on from the Seebohm (1968) recommendations, Schumacher (1974) proposed the thesis that to be too big is undesirable and leads to organisations operating inefficiently. His proposal was small units provide ideal working conditions and more efficient use of resources.

In a study by Meltzer and Salter (1962), of research scientists, it was established that size of organisation and job satisfaction are strongly linked. Meltzer and Salter suggested that satisfaction is greater in medium sized organisations (i.e. about 21—50 persons) than in either large or small organisations. Carpenter (1971) adds weight to this conclusion in his study of classroom teachers. His findings indicate that in medium sized schools (i.e. about 35 employees), job satisfaction is greater than in small or larger schools.

Meltzer and Salter (1962), Carpenter (1971) and Schumacher (1974) are referring to the optimum size of a task culture oriented organisation. The actual size of a task group within the organisation should probably be between 4—7 persons, with a number of task groups operating side by side.

If the total number of employees go beyond 50 persons, then the above studies indicate that a task oriented culture would no longer be dominant.

An alternative approach has been taken, away from the idea of job satisfaction and more approaching the issue from the standpoint of stress felt by the individual in the organisation. Kahn *et al* (1964) states that stress is low in organisations of under 50 persons, but can reach quite intolerable levels in large organisations (i.e. 1,000 persons plus). Kahn refers to organisations that have to come to terms with different cultures and the effect that can have on people. Unfortunately, stress cannot be eradicated by simply just shrivelling organisations to a smaller size. Not only would the economic consequences of such a move be disastrous, but further, for public service organisations who have generated an expected demand of their activities from other organisations and people in the community, they may then not be able to meet their basic commitments.

An alternative would be to give sub-units more autonomy. Kahn discovered that one reason for stress in large organisations is the need for co-ordination amongst many members. By giving sub-units more autonomy, stress is diminished as co-ordination requirements have been reduced. This would in many ways alleviate the stress that people at the top of an organisation may feel. An important part of their job is control and control is more than likely impossible for any one man or set of men at the top. This is not because they are incompetent, but rather that events and conditions are too complex for anyone to comprehend totally and act upon quickly.

However, since Kahn and his group developed their studies, further research indicate that with decentralisation comes greater co-ordination and there is always the danger that co-ordination of the sub-units could become impossible. The sub-units of large organisations could engage in activities that are out of the control and co-ordinative power of those at the top of the organisation.

Cooper and Marshall (1978) support the notion that by simply decentralising, stress will not be alleviated. They conclude that role conflict, role ambiguity, poor relationships with superiors and sub-ordinates and lack of career development are the important stress factors the larger an organisation becomes. As indicated in Figure 1.1 they suggest that the complexity of relationships in an organisation and the formal procedural arrangements are important stress factors which become more problematic with ever increasing size.

Complexity of relationships

The officially prescribed relationships in an organisation become complex in medium to large sized organisations as management strives to maintain control. Control cannot simply be forgotten. Managerial control of resources and people in medium to large sized organisations is vital for the efficient operation of that organisation. However, as has already been shown, effective control is virtually impossible for any one individual to totally digest. As direct control becomes problematic, then people pay greater attention to co-ordination. The work of Child (1977) indicates that the larger an organisation becomes the greater the need for co-ordination. Child suggests that up to 1,000 employees, the number of hierarchical levels rises from four to six. Four levels of hierarchy seems to be the average for about 200 employees (this includes the chief executive, departmental heads, supervisors and operatives) and six at around 1,000 people. From there on, the rate of increase of hierarchical levels is not in proportion to increases in growth. Measuring increases in size by the employment of more persons, at 10,000 employees, the norm indicates about seven or eight levels. Figure 1.2 shows the manner in which the number of levels varies with total size from the results of three different surveys

It is no easy task to manage a large organisation and when faced with

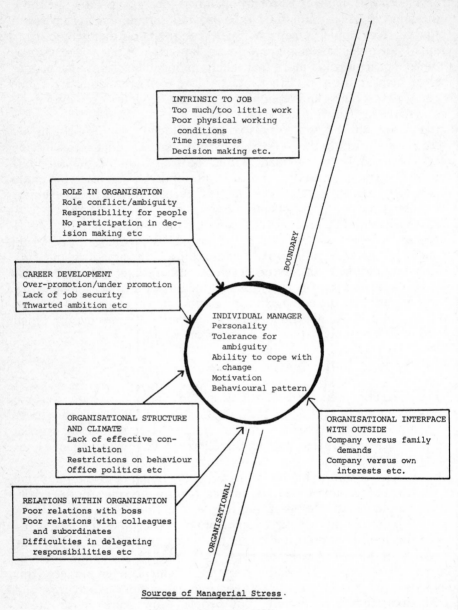

INTRINSIC TO JOB
Too much/too little work
Poor physical working
conditions
Time pressures
Decision making etc.

ROLE IN ORGANISATION
Role conflict/ambiguity
Responsibility for people
No participation in dec-
ision making etc

CAREER DEVELOPMENT
Over-promotion/under promotion
Lack of job security
Thwarted ambition etc

BOUNDARY

INDIVIDUAL MANAGER
Personality
Tolerance for
ambiguity
Ability to cope with
change
Motivation
Behavioural pattern

ORGANISATIONAL STRUCTURE
AND CLIMATE
Lack of effective con-
sultation
Restrictions on behaviour
Office politics etc

ORGANISATIONAL INTERFACE
WITH OUTSIDE
Company versus family
demands
Company versus own
interests etc.

RELATIONS WITHIN ORGANISATION
Poor relations with boss
Poor relations with colleagues
and subordinates
Difficulties in delegating
responsibilities etc

ORGANISATIONAL

Sources of Managerial Stress .

(Cooper and Marshall 1978)

Figure 1.1   Sources of managerial stress

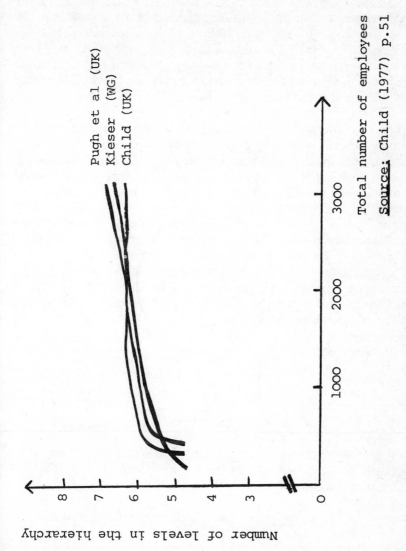

Figure 1.2   The number of hierarchical levels varies with total size — the results of three surveys

substantial problems of control and co-ordination, it is understandable that line managers and administrators easily identify with a role culture. It is equally understandable that task and people oriented professionals neither identify with, nor are sympathetic towards, people who cope with the everyday stresses of managerial administration. One reason for these differences is that role culture oriented managers attempt to determine the shape of the organisation through grouping activities into recognised patterns, an anathema to task culture specialists. Three basic patterns of organisational design are identified: functional structure, divisional structure, and matrix structure. Further, the issue of who maintains control over what, is addressed.

Functional structure In small family business type organisations or small project teams with few employees involved, extensive formal arrangements on how best to structure activities are unnecessary. People know each other sufficiently well not to require an established pattern of roles and responsibilities to determine appropriate behaviour. With growth in size, specialised skills are required which need to be co-ordinated so as to provide an adequate product or service. The functional structure is normally adopted once an organisation develops beyond the small group size. Essentially, activities are grouped into particular departments, with a departmental head, all contributing to an overall common service. The co-ordination of these departments is achieved through the appointment of an overall director, often backed by an executive committee or board.

If the organisation is not too large, there are advantages in employing a functional structure.

1 There is less need for a large number of managers. Because of the relatively simple structure, co-ordination of activities is left to top managers.
2 If particular experts are required to cope with certain problems, it is simpler and cheaper to request assistance from a single department. By grouping particular specialists together in one department then the potential for the efficient utilisation of personnel across the whole organisation is increased.
3 There exist easily recognised and clearly marked career paths for specialists. For the specialist, he enjoys the satisfaction of working with colleagues of similar interests. For the organisation, the hiring and retention of such specialists is simpler as increased pay and status are provided in the career hierarchy. The functional structure neatly combines task and role cultures.

Problems occur in utilising a functional structure once the organisation grows further or diversifies into new products, services or markets. When an organisation grows, diversification is necessary, and this often involves divisionalisation.

Divisional structure Divisionalisation involves splitting the overall organisation into virtually autonomous units whereby each division provides a total service for any one client.

In effect, a number of smaller departments are created within the overall organisation, and these are termed divisions. Each division has at its head a divisional director. Below the divisional directors may exist area directors or officers who may separately accept responsibility for domiciliary and day care, field work and residential care. The distribution of activities at area level is dependant on the size of the authority and the size of the population being serviced in the community. However, as Rowbottom (1974) suggests, the grouping of activities at divisional level will probably be distributed in a functional manner. A number of advantages exist in adopting a divisional structure. These are:

1 Cost and profit issues are the direct responsibility of the divisional directors. The overall director of the organisation is not concerned with the daily finances of the division.
2 The main function of the organisational head quarters is to concern itself with strategic planning, appraisal of policies and projects, and overall financial control. This process involves planning for the future which would be impossible if too many people become involved. Hence, only the divisional directors and possible corporate planning and appraisal specialists in conjunction with the director of the organisation, are involved in considering future developments.
3 Corporate and future planning would be committed to the development of the overall organisation rather than any individual division. It is too simple to identify only with the development of any one division, often to the detriment of other divisions. Hence it is necessary to have a corporate structure above the divisional structures.
4 The ability of a division to respond more freely to particular needs in certain local areas. In essence, self contained units operating within particular geographic localities can meet particular community requirements bearing in mind the budgetary constraints under which they are placed.

Matrix structure The need for matrix structure management arises when an organisation has developed a strong role culture (possibly through divisionalisation) but finds that task culture oriented specialists need to be incorporated more closely with the day to day operation of the

31

organisation. In fact, matrix management is a way of generating task culture oriented attitudes within a role culture organisation.

Matrix structure management arose from the development of the aerospace industry in the USA. The US Government had begun to demand that numerous companies work on large project contracts that required substantial co-ordination and intricate inter-relationship within and between firms. Numerous management and organisation consultants were hired to develop human relations training and develop total organisations into more closely knit teams thereby promoting a more open climate for the total work force. It was recognised that serving two masters, each with quite different objectives and personal values, led to a number of dilemmas within the organisation and a substantial degree of personal stress. Kingdon (1973) states:

> An attempt to combine the advantages of functional specialisation with those of project management, recognising that lateral negotiated relationships, complementary to superior—subordinate authority relationships, are essential for the performance of highly complex and interdependant technical tasks and for the promotion of organisational adaptiveness and flexibility. The key problem is, to derive ways of implementing such relationships and reconciling them with the hierarchical order. (p.1).

For some the matrix management approach may seem contradictory. On the one hand, people do require control and co-ordination in order to work together on quite complex tasks. On the other, control can no longer be applied through hierarchical authority. In an attempt to increase co-ordination at the expense of control, certain public service organisations, including SSD's have introduced an additional role in the structure — the internal consultant. Their purpose is to respond to requests for assistance from persons of any level or organisational unit, if the problem area in question lies within their field of competence.

Whether internal consultants are utilised or not, the distinction between a matrix organisation, a complex organisation and a dis-organised organisation is fundamentally one of attitude, as held by both management and lower level personnel, rather than the presence or absence of rules and regulations. Most organisations function in a matrix manner, but it is the degree of recognition given to matrix development by senior management that is crucial. If higher level management is attempting to impose an authority structure to what is essentially a matrix pattern of work relationships, then the matrix style will predominate but work performance will be poor. Subversive activity at lower levels will take place. Senior management will feel its overall plan is being sabotaged by those beneath and attempt to introduce further controls to, in their terms, rectify the situation.

Eventually, even personnel at middle management level will only pay lip service to formal procedures imposed from above.

From the point of view of persons at lower organisational levels, they will continue to interrelate on a colleague basis in order to meet the requirements of their everyday tasks. The formal procedures imposed from above will be seen as hindrances which have to be by-passed. A substantial amount of time will be lost as senior management will hold numerous meetings to identify ways in which they can, in their eyes, regain control. Those at the lower levels will be meeting to identify ways and means of continuing their work without management interference. In addition to loss of time, trust between persons at different organisational levels will diminish and conflict oriented relationships may become the most common form of interaction. Matrix organisations for the most part are a sign of maturity of the personnel in the organisation rather than a type of organisational structure.

Maintaining control Whatever structure is implemented managers need to maintain some control over daily activities. The way such control works is through procedures, rules, regulations and supervisors.

For task culture oriented professionals, formality of procedure can conjure images of an individual being limited in the sense that his/her expected behaviour is pre-programmed by the organisation. Unless control is poorly applied, that is not the case. Rules and procedures are merely a means of managing contingencies faced by the organisation. Their presence is not solely to limit individual discretion but an attempt to regulate activities so that they are in accord with the expectations established in policies, plans and targets. Problems only arise when middle level managers (role culture) and senior management (possible power culture) become too concerned with maintaining their own position and attempt to reduce, what they would see as, adverse information about their behaviour reaching them. When management wishes to reduce the amount of feedback it receives about its performance, it does so through over-controlling the activities of others.

Over-control could generate passive resistance amongst employees. In situations of over-control, creativity and initiative are dampened and people become unable and unwilling to generate new ideas or pass information up and down the hierarchical line. If employees are unexpectedly called upon to cope with crises, they may find it a difficult, if not impossible, a task. Most certainly, under these conditions, the ability of project groups to work together is limited as creativity and initiative are not required by the organisation. People who strongly identify with a task oriented culture would leave and the remainder would probably continue to operate but ineffectively.

To balance the picture, it must be stressed that the larger an organisation becomes, so the need for control and co-operation increases.

Therefore, it is competently applied control that generates a feeling of motivation in individuals. Task culture oriented groups can be stimulated by role culture oriented managers. Simply, well applied controls do provide for adequate feedback on performance in the doing of tasks. Precise controls are required in budgeting and in the work of lower level operatives. In these cases, people know what they have to accomplish, over what tasks and procedures they are to be assessed and what the likely outcomes of adequate task performance will be. Employees do not feel that the controls imposed are either illegitimate or threatening, but in fact provide positive guidelines for further work.

The greater the need for well applied control, the greater the need for competent supervision.

Competent supervisory activity in any organisation is vital. Most certainly, policy decisions taken by senior management are necessary for the survival of an organisation. But so is competent supervision providing a quality control service that ensures maintenance of required standards of work output. The aim of supervisory activity is to provide a check on the quality of work undertaken by employees but further to act as a referral agent and counsellor in allowing employees to talk through certain work problems that have to be overcome.

Both in a task culture and role culture, supervision is important. In the task culture, the role of the supervisor is more open to both praise and criticism, as co-ordination of widely disparate activities, is required. In addition, personal interaction with others is necessary, emphasising the need for displaying competent interpersonal skills on the part of the supervisor. Supervisors with poor interpersonal skills can be partly responsible for a loss of employee motivation, poor co-ordination and lack of communication between units.

In a role culture system, the situation is somewhat different in that the supervisor fundamentally provides a quality control service ensuring that the rules and procedures laid down by the organisation are adhered to. A role culture organisation, by its very nature requires rules and regulations to ensure adequate control and co-ordination. The aim of supervisors is to ensure compliance with the existing procedural arrangements. Such a situation has implications for the number of persons that can be attached to one supervisor. If work is highly formalised, then the likely span of control of supervisors over employees is likely to be higher in terms of number of persons involved, than in a less formalised work setting. This can be quite an efficient manner of operation especially if specialists support staff are available to the supervisor.

Problems arise, however, in a de-centralised system or where substantial co-ordination of ill-fitting activities is required. Drawing on a range of specialised skills in such situations will be common features of working life. Spans of control will have to be kept narrow, possibly with fairly frequent changeover of supervisory personnel to continually stimulate the process of innovation. The total number of supervisory personnel in such organisations will be large.

Professional v organisational values

Overcoming problems concerned with the size of an organisation or with the complexity of relationships within it, does not guarantee that management will face fewer problems. Beyond and above questions of work organisation is the fundamental issue of personal values. With what do people identify? For example, a task oriented professional would consider himself as operating at a higher level of personal competence and mental capacity than a role oriented administrator. In order to maintain a high level of performance, most professionals would identify reasonably strongly with a professional ethos. The more an individual identifies with a particular set of values, the more his actions are guided by those values and the more he becomes unmanageable from an organisational point of view.

Consider the key factors determining professionalism (Table 1.5).

Table 1.5

Key factors determining professionalism

Control	Moral identity	Time
1. Knowledge exclusive to a few people.	1. Persons of similar personal values put their views into practise.	1. Certain groups withstand criticism and remain intact over long periods of time.
2. Communal recognition in the sense of standing distinctly apart from other groups in employment.		2. Once established, the group develops a commonly recognised professional identity (sometimes distinguished as holding only part professional status).
3. Prescribed standards of service over task activities and interpersonal relationships.		

First, the issue of *control* of persons acting in a professional capacity and of the tasks they can and cannot perform, is most important. As can be seen in Table 1.5 the control of professional persons is

35

expressed in three different ways; knowledge that is exclusive to relatively few persons; recognition from key members of the community that a particular group provides a unique service distinctly apart from other groups in employment; controlling procedures identified and enforced by the professional body, stipulating what are and what are not appropriate standards of service.

Second, *moral identity* is a strong influence on the behaviour of people. By entering a profession, an opportunity exists for persons of compatable personal values to put into practice their view of how things ought to be.

Third, survival over long periods of *time* is crucial. Groups that describe their activities as being professional and are able to withstand outside criticism and remain intact over long periods, are eventually recognised by the community as providing some sort of professional service. Apart from groups as doctors and lawyers, where little disagreement exists as to their professional identity, a number of occupations (for example estate agents, social workers and even teachers) are now generally recognised as holding professional status. The development of estate agents, social workers and other groups has involved a struggle to gain professional identity over a period of a number of years.

Two strong influences on how to behave appropriately at work are simultaneously in operation — the influence of the profession and the influence of the organisation. It is fairly accurate to state that any group of people who aspire to espoused professional status and are employed by a large organisation, hold different priorities as to how to put their beliefs into practise. The beliefs of a professionally oriented society as BASW and any SSD are likely to be similar. It is however, the ordering of priorities that leads to conflict. When and how quickly things should be done, leads to as much disagreement as what things should be done.

Take for example, the difference in behaviour between a task culture oriented professionally qualified social worker and role culture oriented, equally professionally qualified, middle or senior manager (area officer/assistant director) over the question of identifying new needs in the community. The task culture oriented social worker would value identifying new problem areas, quickly becoming involved with identified problem cases and if necessary, publicising any new developments through the local or even mass media. Individuals who identify more closely with their employing organisation would behave far more cautiously. Identifying new problem areas in the community could create political difficulties in the relationship between elected counsellors and the full time officers. Further, certain problems in the community could provide the unwelcome attention of the press which may put considerable strain on senior management.

Ironically, most senior managers in SSDs have been practising social workers in the early stages of their career but in order to perform competently in their current positions, it would be necessary to have adjusted their personal values to those synonymous with a role culture. Both social workers and professionally qualified senior managers are likely to wish to achieve the same end objectives. It is the way those objectives are to be achieved and the time taken, that can lead to basic disagreements.

An added complication exists, namely that some aspiring professional groups may be more dependent on their employing organisation than they would wish to acknowledge.

It is recognised that a number of groups in society who aspire towards full professional status fail to achieve full professional recognition. Etzioni (1964) offered the concept of a semi-profession and thereby introduced a middle position between the particular demands of occupational groups (teachers, nurses, social workers) and the response of 'society at large'.

Etzioni states that the semi-professions are as groups new professions, which differ from the more traditional, as law and medicine, in the following ways: training is of a shorter time scale; the right to privileged communication is less established; there exists a poorly recognised specialised body of knowledge; less control is exercised over members of the community who seek the services of the occupational group.

Consider some of the constraints that social work practitioners have to face. Social workers, have to relate to supervisors who provide a quality control service over their task activities. Organisational authority is vested in the supervisory role in order to both guide and control the work of the social worker in the field. Hence, the right to privileged communication and individual choice of action is limited.

A further restraint identified by Etzioni is the inability of a semi-profession to generate its own body of knowledge. In the field of medicine there exist university or teaching hospitals which generate, teach and apply knowledge through professionals who make the generation of such knowledge the organisation's goals. However, with social work this is not the case — why? In the first instance, active practitioners with case loads do not lead SSDs. Those that do occupy senior positions in the social services are basically administrators and not casework practitioners. Consequently, their work orientation and goals are towards functioning within the administrative arrangements. These are for the best reasons — in order to provide an adequate social work service within the present public service organisations. Second, the work of field practitioners is confined to the communication and application of particular fields of specialisation and not the generation of an exclusive body of knowledge. Under these circumstances, how does the relationship between the task culture semi-professional and the organisation develop? Two themes have emerged from a number of studies.

First, the work of writers such as Maniha (1974), Gaston (1975), Algie (1973a; 1973b) and Green (1975) indicates a potentially problematic relationship between organisational growth and the increasing number of professional or semi-professional specialists employed in the organisation.

A serious problem that senior policy making managers have to face, is that with increasing professional job specialisation comes a tendency for specialists to pull in different directions. This is partly due to a wish for functional autonomy according to each specialists' particular training and personal values, and also because involvement in singularly complex work leads to a narrowing of understanding of the total organisation perspective. Essentially, complex specialists have been identified as having a poorly developed sense of understanding of the overall pattern of organisational policy.

Hence, a second problem area emerges that of lack of confidence between line and staff personnel, in each others ability to manage work problems. One argument for the growth of specialisation is that line management could delegate certain tasks to staff specialists. But this is dependant on line staff having sufficient confidence in the abilities of the specialists available. Warham (1977) and Greenwood (1965) indicate that a true professional specialist would have little difficulty in establishing such a trusting relationship as his particular knowledge base and social status would naturally require that certain work be referred in his direction. For example, a medical officer employed by an organisation would fall into this category. However, it is those jobs that Etzioni has identified as semi-professional, where problems arise between specialist and line managers. Problems arise because line management recognises that the specialist does not work from an exclusive knowledge base and partly because management itself has different objectives to the specialist.

Other writers have developed the theme of the semi-professional *v.* bureaucracy from the point of view of a positive relationship between the person and the organisation. Hasenfeld (1972) and Van Maanen (1978) indicate that it is possible to achieve full professional status from being a semi-professional in people processing organisations, employment agencies, etc. Attaining professional status is due more to the influence of the large organisation as opposed to the knowledge base of professional activity. Kohn (1971) indicates that it would be impossible to behave as a professional without the support of a well established and co-ordinated organisation. Kohn supports the notion that the more bureaucratic an organisation becomes in terms of establishing procedures for numerous activities, identifying job roles, preparing formal job descriptions and developing a commonly understood hierarchical pattern, the greater the confidence the professional specialist will have to act in various situations.

It is unlikely that social services can ever escape the classical professional/bureaucratic conflict, for SSDs are organisations where a mix of cultures is probably the norm. By not having a simplistically structured organisation to manage, greater emphasis has to be placed on the managerial skills of line managers in SSDs. Line managers have to be able to develop an acceptable working relationship with the community oriented practitioner. The key to the relationship is trust; trust in terms of personal competence and trust in terms of recognising and accepting the other party's different personal values. If trust exists between the line manager and the community oriented practitioner, then co-operation over fulfilling social work tasks and organisational demands will follow. If trust does not exist, as both Gowler and Parry (1979) and Garner (1979) suggest does not in the NHS, then eventually both the organisation and client groups will suffer.

Summary

The four key organisational cultures of power, task, role and person are identified. It is noted that any one or more of these cultures can be prevalent in an organisation at any one moment in time. The salient features of each culture are identified in terms of differences in organisation structure; leadership practise; the degrees of challenge and responsibility, warmth and support; reward and punishment; the setting and assessing of performance standards; the degree of conflict and the ability of employees to identify with the organisation. It is shown that substantial differences exist between people who identify with different cultures, in both their attitudes to work, the employing organisation and work behaviour.

Changes of organisation structure influence the existing cultures within an organisation. Increasing the total size of the organisation can lead to problems of control and co-ordination of activities. Equally, increases in size can lead to a substantial number of employees experiencing various forms of work stress.

It is postulated that increases in size lead to greater emphasis on role cultures than task cultures as organisational relationships become more complex. In fact, greater attention is given to analysing and developing organisational relationships than professional or personal relationships. Such a situation is likely to lead to clashes between people who identify with professional values and those who identify with organisational values. Not only do the two groups identify with different work practices, but further could find it difficult to agree on the priorities given to certain activities in attempting to achieve similar objectives.

Despite attempts to make organisation structures more diverse, it is such differences in work practice that lead to a state of permanent potential conflict.

2 Re-organisation and the rise of bureaucracy

How to manage the personal services has until recently been a neglected subject. Little or no attention was given to how to manage people, how to manage information, what should be done in planning for the future and how were personal service organisations to become more effective in meeting their objectives. The reason for this is that the study of any social service type organisation has fundamentally been the preserve of the political scientists whose particular frame of reference is, and has been, to try and understand whole systems as they have developed from the past and what should be their purpose for the future. In so doing, studies of public bureaucracies have tended to highlight the relatively stable features of administrative systems and attempt to explain modifications of these features through the impact of various factors such as political change, cultural and value changes in society. Some academics as Biller (1971) for example, find that public organisations have ambiguous relationships with the external societal environment, which is subject to re-definition by elected politicians and is thus more turbulent than the external environment of private organisations. He suggests that fundamental irreconcilable differences exist between the public and private sectors. In this he is supported by Baker (1972) and Buchanan (1975) on the grounds that public organisations do not have clear goals and are not disciplined by a market economy. Crozier (1968) disagrees, for whilst acknowledging that technical and economic constraints are not so well defined for public organisations as for private organisations, there is a growing convergence of these two types of organisations, since recent technical innovations permit the costing of so considered, unquantifiable data (i.e. planning, programming, budgeting systems). The rational treatment of information now imposes a scientific discipline on civil servants. Thus, the margin for political negotiation which has characterised public bureaucracies will be reduced, and they will approach private organisations in terms of corporate strategy, organisation structures and internal functioning *visa vie* decision making processes.

Accordingly, most work on public bureaucracies has not been concerned with specific organisational models and practises on how systems can be organised or re-organised to work better, but rather holistic, all embracing issues which have been the foundation of political science. Social services and local government re-organisation introduced new thinking to this field. A direct outcome of social services and local government re-organisation was an increase in the size of local government units and the implication of that, was a search for organisational models that would suit the new streamlined units. Fundamentally, greater emphasis was placed on management and administration.

Re-organisation

Developing appropriate administrative models has been the centre of discussion (in Great Britain) for the last decade in the social services. Such interest was stimulated by a basic assumption of Seebohm (1968) that any re-planning of community social services had to be accompanied by fundamental administrative re-organisation.

The principal contribution of the Seebohm report was that the activities of the former childrens', welfare and health departments (where the latter specialised in mental health) should be joined into the same administrative hierarchy, the social service department. The rationalisation that social work activity would be best placed under one roof, generated not unexpectedly, discussion on managerial and organisational matters. The matters concentrated on two major areas — organisation structure and the planning process.

Organisation structure

The warnings

Earlier publications concluded that wherever possible, organisational structures should not fall into the 'bureaucratic trap' by having tall hierarchies (Hopkins 1969) but should be flexible (Algie 1970) and adaptable to changing conditions (Barter 1969).

One group emerged whose research and consultancy activities provided the blue-prints of the various types of organisation structures appropriate for the social services even up to the present day. The outstanding contributors are Kogan *et al* (1971) and Rowbottom *et al* (1974) and the BIOSS research teams.[1]

The BIOSS teams are probably the major influence to one of the most extensive and significant organisational change programmes of the decade. Heavily involved in the re-organisation of the Health Services (Kogan *et al* 1971), the team applied itself to investigating the problems caused by the rapid growth, in terms of organisational size, of the personal services.

The results are in a series of publications, typified by the works of Kogan and Rowbottom. The Kogan blue-prints for organising a social service department are a concise text discussing the following four points:

a) patterns of organisation of SSDs;
b) objectives and operational activities of SSDs;
c) the overall structure of SSDs and their relationship with area teams;
d) social workers and accountability.

A social service organisation as such is not defined, but the text refers to definitions of working relationships established at BIOSS. It is accepted that the policies of an organisation are expressions of intention, and that intentions and recommendations are brought into practise by the authority's executive programme.[2] All policies should be precise statements called objectives which must have meaning when stated as operational and non-operational activities. Operational activities are defined as activities which must be pursued by the department if their objectives are to be fulfilled or modified. Essentially, an operational activity is the care, therapy, protection or evaluation activity concerned with case work, group work or community work. Once activities have been determined they are sub-divided into more precise groups of tasks. Tasks are defined as assignments of work to be undertaken within specified resources and time limits. Tasks are then allocated to particular roles or teams and Kogan (1971:26) states that:

---

1 BIOSS is an abbreviation for the Brunel Institute of Organisation and Social Studies.
2 By executive, Newman & Rowbottom (1968) mean a system of people in the structure of work roles — the executive system. This includes people in roles at all levels and is the means whereby the work of the organisation is carried out.

the creation of these divisions is important in deciding how to differentiate the tasks undertaken by the area team and those undertaken by the specialist and centralised teams.

Non-operational activities are the administrative and personnel work, such as recruitment, selection, training, arranging for pensions, sick-leave etc, which support the operational activities. The distinction between operational and non-operational is made so that organisational members can be clear as to the objectives or outcomes of decisions they make. Second, task divisions of operational and non-operational help to identify the authority and accountability relationships in the department. (Fig. 2.1.)

The two terms, authority and accountability are important themes for most of the BIOSS research work. Authority is defined as: the authority carried in the role which is the right to use resources at discretion including the resource of other people to do work. (Kogan 1971:60)

Accountability is identified as being the way that the role holder is answerable for how he had exercised his authority (Kogan 1971:60). Authority and accountability are both properties of roles. Thereby under these prescriptions, an efficient organisation depends on structural factors in the sense of having competent people in pre-determined roles. Based on these two definitions, a number of organisational relationships have been identified, such as superior—subordinate relationship : staff relationship : collateral relationships and cross-over point, and these relationships have been arranged to produce a series of organisational outlines.[1]

Kogan provides basic organisational sketches of role relationships for SSDs. Rowbottom goes further, identifying different organisational models, based on different activities which are divided into three broad functional areas (fieldwork; domiciliary and day-care; residential care)

---

1 *A superior—subordinate relationship* arises when A is accountable for certain work and is assigned a subordinate B to assist him in his work.
A is accountable for the work which B does for him.
A is accountable: for helping to select B; for inducting B into his role; for assigning work and allocating resources to B; for appraising B's general performance and ability.
A has authority: to veto the selection of B for the role; to make an official appraisal of B's performance and ability; to decide if B is unsuitable for performing any of the work which A is accountable (Rowbottom *et al* 1974:11—12)
A *staff relationship* arises when special assistance may be required on personnel and organisational matters by a superior in co-ordinating the activities of subordinates. (Kogan *et al* 1971:61)
A *collateral relationship* is one where mutual adjustment and accommodation between colleagues is necessary for each to carry out certain tasks, and where both are members of the executive hierarchy, but neither has the authority to instruct the other (Kogan *et al* 1971:62)
A *cross-over point* is the first common superior in the organisation above any two colleague roles (Kogan *et al* 1971:62)

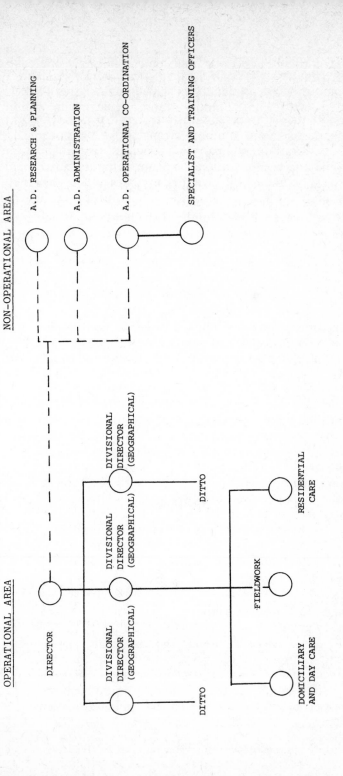

OPERATIONAL AREA

NON-OPERATIONAL AREA

A.D. RESEARCH & PLANNING

A.D. ADMINISTRATION

A.D. OPERATIONAL CO-ORDINATION

SPECIALIST AND TRAINING OFFICERS

DIRECTOR

DIVISIONAL DIRECTOR (GEOGRAPHICAL)

DIVISIONAL DIRECTOR (GEOGRAPHICAL)

DIVISIONAL DIRECTOR (GEOGRAPHICAL)

DITTO

DITTO

DOMICILIARY AND DAY CARE

FIELDWORK

RESIDENTIAL CARE

A.D. - ASSISTANT DIRECTOR

Taken from Rowbottom et al (1974) Social Services Departments p.79

Figure 2.1   Operational and non-operational specialism in a divisional structure

or on geographical spread, whereby any single organisational division can deal with any client problems. In the divisional model, a number of relatively autonomous sub-departments exist within the larger SSD. It was thought that with either model, most departments would incorporate between five to nine levels of hierarchy (Rowbottom and Hey 1973).

An additional organisational model is that of the matrix organisation which involves a hierarchical structure whereby certain roles are co-ordinative in addition to being managerial (Rowbottom *et al* 1974:32). This approach to matrices does not replace but is intended to comple-ment hierarchical structures. For example, the role of the principal or consultant social worker will give a matrix outlook to a hierarchical structure.

Planning process

Inevitably, accompanying the growth in size came the need to plan. The services that any SSD provides are numerous and cannot be left to happen by chance. For example, two types of operational services have to be considered:

1 *Macro-level services* aimed at the total community which include;

   a) developing voluntary agencies and activities;
   b) developing self-help groups;
   c) registration and inspection of voluntary organisations and agencies;
   d) identifying new areas of need;
   e) informing the public of services available;
   f) informing the public of their rights.

2 *Micro-level services* aimed at individuals which include;

   a) casework with children and families;
   b) casework with particular individuals in need e.g. alcoholics; drug addicts;
   c) providing information and advice;
   d) supervisory activities;
   e) arranging for services as money, goods, meals, accom-modation, transport, recreations, aids and adaptations, medical and paramedical treatment, occupational train-ing, adoption agency services, sheltered employment and so the list continues according to the problems in each authority.

In addition, there exist the non-operational services such as:

a) research and evaluation, which involves identifying areas of social distress which are not being adequately catered for; in addition identifying new areas of social distress;
b) strategic planning which involves planning in conjunction with other statutory, private or voluntary organisations;
c) public relations which involves maintaining contact with the press and giving lectures in the community;
d) staffing and training;
e) managerial tasks such as the induction of staff, distribution of work, supervision of work, appraisal of personnel, staff development etc.;
f) finance which involves all matters concerned with accounting, budgeting and budgetary control;
g) logistic consideration which involves providing adequate premises and equipment, materials and any other support services required for operational work to be done.
h) secretarial.

It was the Baines Report (1972) that emphasised the need for planning and provided a distinction between managing existing operating plans to do with the rational application of existing resources to existing work practices (short-term planning) and the development of intentions for the future (long-term planning).

Baines states that the link between short-term and long-term planning is the responsibility of the chief executive of the local authority. His role is identified as essentially that of co-ordinator in being primarily the leader of a team of chief officers, some of whom may sit on the chief officers management team. In addition, the chief executive sits on the policy and resources committee, which has the three responsibilities of central control and finance, advising the council on future plans and objectives, and co-ordinating the implementation of those plans.

The purpose of creating the chief officers management team is to ensure that the authority as a whole would be considered and discussed by all of the professional interests before decisions are taken. The objective is joint problem solving and the medium is discussion through the exchange of views and opinions within the team. Similar to the Kogan and Rowbottom proposals, alternative management structures are offered by Baines. Fundamentally, two alternative structures are recommended. The structure in Figure 2.2 indicates that there are no senior chief officers who may have authority over other chief officers. They would be called on to assist the management team on matters within their sphere of responsibility. Figure 2.3 illustrates an alternative structure whereby some departments are grouped together under directors, with only some of the chief officers being members of the management team.

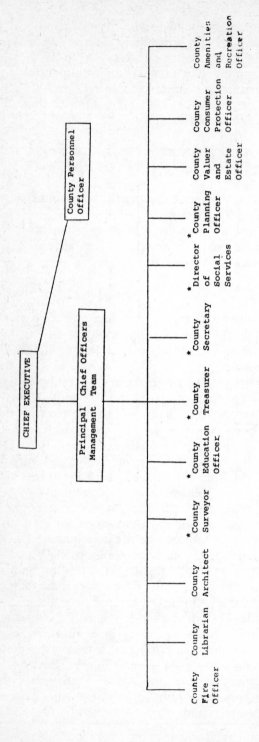

CHIEF EXECUTIVE

County Personnel Officer

Principal Chief Officers Management Team

County Fire Officer

County Librarian

County Architect

* County Surveyor

* County Education Officer

* County Treasurer

* County Secretary

* Director of Social Services

* County Planning Officer

County Valuer and Estate Officer

County Consumer Protection Officer

County Amenities and Recreation Officer

* Members of management team

Figure 2.2   Departmental structure — non-metropolitan county

48

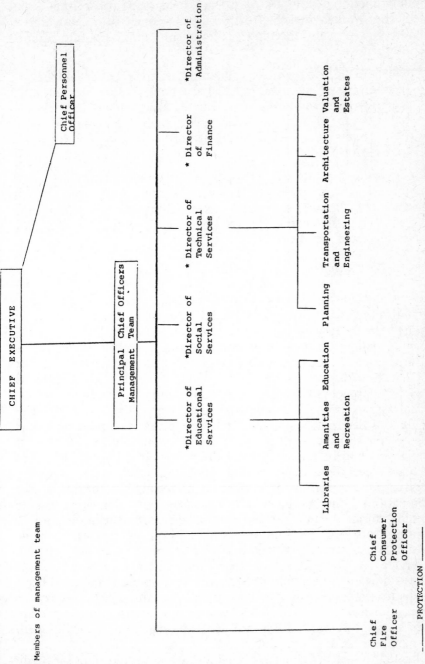

Figure 2.3   Departmental structure — non-metropolitan county

49

Baines recommends that for longer term planning, the corporate planning function be established. Corporate planning to a certain degree is achieved through the chief officers management team. However, to facilitate this process, the report recommends that corporate planners be appointed who,

> will be concerned with bringing together the plans developed by the various divisions, but will also conduct special studies where required, monitor achievements against plans and help to determine the appropriate long-range objectives and near-term targets at which we (the authority) should be aiming. (p. 84 para. 7.26.)

What is being suggested is that people be appointed to roles whose function will be to assess the long-term objectives and plans of the authority as a whole. This would involve facilitating better relationships amongst chief officers and further, spending a substantial amount of time with elected members.

What use is planning?

Long-term planning, the ability to foresee the future and make adequate preparation have been held as the prime functions of senior management in local government. However, as Falk and Lee (1978) indicate, planning may well be desirable, but in reality, global surveys and ten year plans have quickly been jettisoned. The personal services have had to adjust to a freeze on expenditure which has required them to adopt approaches to expenditure control under crisis circumstances. In contrast, traditional planning approaches were all geared to growth.

Falk and Lee rightly state that ten year plans were based on a single set of assumptions, centred around the extrapolation of trends from the past in order to be able to predict the future. It is impossible to plan for macro-level services as if they were micro-level services. What is necessary is not merely extrapolation of trends but further, a close examination of the key issues which face us today. The great value of planning is that it can assist decision makers clarify the implications of adopting different assumptions, focusing on choices that involve alternative ends and means and making assessments as to the well being of service recipients based on that choice. Such an approach would involve individuals or groups holding different opinions and deciding on the distribution of costs and benefits, largely through the exercise of power. Consequently, who is and who is not involved in the planning process, who is and who is not participating in or controlling the planning process, are important issues.

Planning is not just a means of gathering appropriate data for prediction purposes, but more a personal philosophy about how many people's opinions should one heed; who and how many persons should be involved in active decision making, and the simple recognition that planning can often be an expression of intent of particular groups.

So where are we now?

On the positive side, re-organisation brought social service administration away from the stifling philosophy of the political scientists. Constantly debating political norms and values achieves little when considering the problems of social service implementation. Therefore re-organisation began a debate over issues as to the appropriate organisation design, structure and size for the effective implementation of any social welfare service. On the negative side, re-organisation increased the size of social service organisations but did little towards stimulating major developments in social casework practise.

Over the last fifteen years, change has generally been an important theme for the public services in England and Wales. The Salmon Report (1966) heralded the change era by attempting to rationalise the nursing hierarchy according to specific definitions of nursing tasks and grades of pay. Seebohm followed suit, recommending that any improvements in the social services had to be accompanied by fundamental administrative re-organisation. Within two years, the Local Government Act 1972 was in operation, requiring substantial changes in local government boundaries and the re-allocation of local government duties within the new units. The reason for the change of local government boundaries was admirable: to create an equitable system whereby local government units could meet the demands of comparable population sizes. A year later, the Health Services were reformed in order to establish comparable geographic boundaries with the newly existent local government units.

The striking similarity between the four major change programmes is the emphasis on administrative rationality and the seemingly subconscious belief that reform of internal management structures would eventually lead to improvements in the health, care and satisfaction of the public at large. As I indicated in a recent paper (Kakabadse and Worrall 1978), not only are Maud (1967), Mallaby (1968) and Baines (1972) similar in their recommendations on management structures for local government but are virtually identical to the proposals of the Health Services Green Paper (1970). Overall two types of recommendations were proposed:

a) the necessity to have clear hierarchies, easily recognisable spans of control and unity of command;

b) the desirability of the corporate management philosophy in order to overcome ad-hocery, departmentalism and attain a positive attitude toward long-term planning in relation to viewing the local authority (or Area Health Authority) as a total unit.

The one question that was not asked during the periods of re-organisation and is not even being confronted today, is: are the structures in use conducive to developing the operational social work tasks of SSDs? Simply, can social work activities be competently developed in the existing structures by personnel who are required to be sufficiently motivated to meet client demands and organisational requirements? The answer to the question depends on the attitudes that have developed towards professional practice and the employing department on the part of staff members. The question is fully examined in Chapter 3.

Summary

The management of the social services has been a largely neglected subject until the Seebohm proposals which recommended major changes in the organisational structure of the personal services. The BIOSS group at Brunel University responded to the challenge by sketching out ideal organisational structures that would meet the needs of the new SSD. Role and functional relationships were defined and in meeting the requirements of the new department due to increases in size, greater complexity of organisational relationships was the result.

The need to plan was emphasised by both the BIOSS group and the Baines Report as the provision of services had become intricate and costly. In the Baines Report, planning was related to organisation structures rather than exploring the process of planning. In contrast, other writers have stated that an integral part of the process of planning involves both ensuring adequate provision for the future and understanding the problems that individuals and units have to face today. Such thinking requires more of a problem solving attitude as opposed to creating an organisational structure for planning.

In fact, change for the public services over the last 15 years has concentrated on creating organisation structures to cope with increases in organisation size. Whether the current structures are conducive to the practise of social work or whether the relationship between the task oriented professional social worker and his employing department leads to the development of positive attitudes towards community social work practice, is something that needs to be determined.

3 Studies of organisation culture in SSDs

The studies described in this chapter concentrate on examining the work attitudes, personal values and norms and the on-the-job learning processes, that personnel from all levels in SSDs experience as part of their working life. From the results of the studies, it will be possible to begin to understand some of the strengths and weaknesses inherent in today's SSDs. The studies described in this chapter are dependent on one basic assumption; the true driving force behind any organisation is its personnel. It is the attitudes that people develop towards their work, peers, superiors, clients and the total organisation itself, that distinguishes an effective from an ineffective organisation.

I and colleagues have conducted a number of separate studies for a period of over five years, analysing the organisation culture of twelve SSDs. The studies are presented in six separate categories:

a) Key stages of the research programme;
b) Study of organisation structure;
c) Studies of culture at the organisation level;
d) Studies of culture at the group level;
e) Studies of culture at the individual level;
f) Mix of cultures (interpretation of the research findings).

The various stages that we as a research team went through, are interesting. We recognised at the outset that we had to appreciate the key issues that determined the attitudes and work behaviours of personnel in SSDs. To achieve this, we adopted an action research approach. We attempted to become involved in the work life of certain people in certain departments.

This led us to realise that the distinction between organisation, group and individual was important. The reason that our findings are presented in such a way, is that we noticed that the respondents in the original sample population gave different and seemingly contradictory accounts. Views concerning the total organisation were somewhat different to peoples' perceptions concerning group behaviour and different again when individuals talked personally about their work behaviour and attitudes. Consequently, the research findings are presented in much the same way that the participants in the study seemed to present their views. In the final section of this chapter, interpretations of the findings are offered.

Key stages of the research

First stage

Stage 1 of the study was primarily to ascertain what job and organisationally related issues would be relevant to social services personnel. Negotiations were undertaken with a north west metropolitan district authority and permission was granted to carry out a series of interviews in the social services department. Current staff lists were sent to the researcher who sampled personnel for interview according to role, thereby ensuring that all levels within the department were represented. Any people in roles not duplicated, either due to the authority inherent in the role or task specialism (for example, the director of the department, or the assistant director of residential services) were chosen for interview and letters of appointment sent to the appropriate personnel. Where more than one person filled the role (for example, generic social worker field level) a sample was taken, and the persons chosen requested to interview (N=50).[1] The interviews were unstructured with respondents speaking into a tape recorder. The issues to emerge concerned the standardisation and proliferation of rules in the department — the formalisation of procedures; the process of decision-making; the degree of participation in decision-making; social relations and the development of specialist and functional task groups.

Second stage

The three basic issues to arise from the first set of interviews in the SSD concerned rules, decision making, and the impersonal nature of

1   N indicates the number of respondents in the study. Hence, N=50 means fifty people were interviewed.

interpersonal relations. A questionnaire was drafted which measured each of these issues and was incorporated in the main study. I was interested in developing a fourth dimension, namely how do people adjust to working within their current organisation structure, even if they find it unfavourable. One way would be to understand the supporting or constraining influences that each individual experiences in his job (Payne 1975). The Organisational Supports or Constraints Questionnaire, originally drafted by Roy Payne (Sheffield University) was piloted by myself (the questionnaire had not been tested on any population beforehand). The instrument was distributed amongst hospital administrators, nursing personnel, and polytechnic staff, (see Appendix 2), around the Manchester conurbation (N=252), with stamped, addressed envelopes for reply. The results were statistically analysed and in addition, the respondents were asked to make comments about the questionnaire on a separate paper attached. From the comments and the statistical analysis, the final questionnaire for the main study was prepared.

Third stage: the main study

The main study was concerned with assessing the relationship between certain properties of organisation structure and aspects of organisation culture, including one dimension of job climate (i.e. the supporting or constraining influences that a person experiences whilst doing his or her job). Originally, more variables were incorporated in the design but a number did not survive statistical analysis. Each of the dimensions measured in this study are listed below:

1 Properties of organisation structure[1] —
   a) centralisation;
   b) formalisation;
   c) complexity;
   d) routiness of work.

2 Properties of organisation culture[1] —
   a) job autonomy;
   b) career fulfilment;
   c) questioning authority;
   d) interpersonal aggression;
   e) team performance rating index (measure of organisational identity).

---

1 The research of Hage and Aiken (1967a; 1967b; 1969) and the work of Payne and Phesey (1971) helped me not only in formulating my ideas but also gave me the opportunity to replicate some of their studies to compare my results with theirs.

3 Properties of group culture —
   a) job support/constraint for staff;
   b) job support/constraint for supervisors;
   c) job support/constraint for managers.

In addition, certain factual variables were incorporated, collating information on the age and size of each department. Survey interview schedules (i.e. questionnaires) were used; with separate schedules for managers, supervisors and staff. The schedules (questionnaires) were not self administered. Each question was read out to the respondents who answered according to the appropriate card presented to them. There were five cards, and on each card was printed the range of responses appropriate to the question asked. The scales and questions are given in Appendices 1 and 2.

Whilst the study was being planned, the possibility of utilising a mail questionnaire approach was considered. The suggestion was quickly rejected because of the unpredictable nature of responses. Once the idea of mail questionnaires was rejected, the voluntary co-operation of the respondents was given priority for the survey approach. As the respondents were not to see the questionnaire schedule, and hence, had no idea of item order or conceptual meaning, the schedules were so drafted to ensure minimal confusion for the respondents when changing from one response card to the next. Consequently, items were placed in sequence, according to the scale response intervals and 'common sense' categorisation.

The data was collected from nine social service organisations located in North-West England, most of them located in the Manchester conurbation. All the organisations had above 800 employees providing the state regulated services such as psychiatric care, child placement, child care, care for the elderly, institutional care, emergency services. Some of the organisations offered additional community and welfare development services.

All initial negotiations for entry into each SSD were carried out with the director of each department. Etzioni (1970) argues that the only way to enter any client system is with the permission of the executive strata. On obtaining the necessary permission, we requested up-to-date staff lists for sampling. Each department was divided into levels and job occupants were selected randomly within these categories; in other words a stratified random sample based on a key dimension of the department—managerial levels. Thus, the approach adopted corresponded to the way the organisations were structured, and hence to the reality of organisational life. Respondents within each department were selected by the following criteria:

   a) all executives and departmental heads;
   b) all supervisory personnel who held specialist posts;

c) in departments of less than twenty professionals (including supervisors not in category b), one half being selected randomly;

d) one-third selected randomly in departments of more than 20 professionals.

Non-professional in the sense of administrative and maintenance personnel were not interviewed as they were less likely to be involved in the establishment of organisational goals and policies. Job occupants in the upper levels were selected because they are most likely to be key decision makers and determine organisational policy, whereas job occupants in the lower levels were selected randomly. We attempted to ensure that everyone in a professional role (whether managerial or social work) was represented even though numerous people (especially at the lower levels) may be occupying similar roles, (for example, field social workers). The different ratios within the departments ensured that smaller departments were adequately represented. The stratified design resulted in 47 interviews in the smallest department, to 130 in the largest, leading to a total of 603 respondents.

Fourth stage

Once the major questionnaire study was complete, the final follow-up stage of unstructured interviewing began. Concentrating on only two metropolitan district authorities, in-depth unstructured interviews were held with personnel from all levels of the organisation. Similar to stage three, the sampling of personnel for interview was selective to ensure that people in all roles in the organisations were represented at interview.

The purpose of these interviews was to understand the learning process that individuals of different managerial levels in SSDs go through in doing their everyday tasks. Such learning is more commonly termed, experience, i.e. gaining expertise from doing the job. Consequently some of the issues identified were; what do people consider to be motivating or non-motivating factors in their work; what do they think they can and cannot change in their organisation and what commonly held norms are developing around certain tasks.

From the transcriptions of the interviews, a selective content analysis procedure was undertaken. A sample of interviews from the content analysis is presented, representing responses from social workers, senior social workers, residential officers and those in management posts.

Study of organisation structure in nine SSDs

Based on the discussions at the first unstructured interview stage, four themes seemed to consistently emerge concerning the structure of the departments. The four themes were decision making, rules and procedures, complexity of formal relationships and a feeling of too much routine involved in doing one's daily work. Consequently, the relevant properties of organisation structure adopted for the question-naire study were.[1] —

a) centralisation;
b) formalisation;
c) complexity;
d) routineness of work.

Centralisation is a measure of who makes decisions and over what issues. Two features of centralisation are taken:

1 The degree to which occupants of various positions particip-ate in decisions about the allocation of resources and organisational policies (*index of participation in decision making*).
2 The extent to which employees are assigned tasks and then provided with the freedom to implement them without inter-ruption from supervisors (*index of hierarchy of authority*).

By formalisation is meant the degree to which rules, regulations and procedures are seen to influence the doing of work. Formality is considered to have four aspects:

1 *The index of job regulation* representing the degree to which jobs are formally controlled through the rules and regulations in the department.
2 *The index of rule observation* measuring whether or not these rules are employed. This is a different measure than the index of hierarchy of authority above, for the intention is to see to what extent rules are used, and that is distinctly different to measuring the involvement of superiors in assessing the quality of a subordinate's work.
3 The presence of rules manual(s).
4 The presence of job descriptions.

Complexity is taken to be an aspect of specialisation but the emphasis is on expertise gained by training as opposed to the division and systemisation of daily routine tasks. This property is represented by four measures:

---

1   See Appendix 1 for the Questionnaire on Organisation Structure.

1 The degree of training required by each occupational specialisation.
2 The degree of outside-the-organisation professional activity
associated with each occupation.
3 The number of occupational specialities in the organisation.
4 The degree of trade union activity associated with each
occupation.

The fourth property of *routineness of work* is incorporated as a
measure of how people feel they are doing their work. Are they obliged
to undertake their work in a routine manner or do they have sufficient
flexibility to regulate the manner in which they discharge their daily
duties? (Appendix 1)[1]

Results

The procedure adopted in the next sections to determine the importance of certain structural properties, is to correlate certain of the
properties with the others remaining. In this way, one can draw out a
map indicating the types of organisation structure seen by the
participants to be most significant.

Is participation in decision making important?

Figure 3.1 indicates participation in decision making to be a poor
measure of organisational structure for the nine departments. It has
only one significant correlation and that is a positive association with
the index of professional training. *This suggests that those with greater
formal education and professional training, participate in making
decisions.* As no significant relationship is found with any of the other
properties, it indicates that participation in decision making is determined by the type and degree of training that particular individuals
have undergone. These findings are similar to those of other researchers
into organisations, namely that those better trained, participate in
decisions concerning overall departmental development. Alternatively,
it could be that as the nature of the work of these organisations is
difficult to standardise, employees naturally tend to have greater
involvement with their own individual tasks as opposed to departmental
policies, for they find sufficient satisfaction and scope for innovation
in their work. This alternative proposition is tested in the next section.

1   See Appendix 1 for items on Organisation Structure.

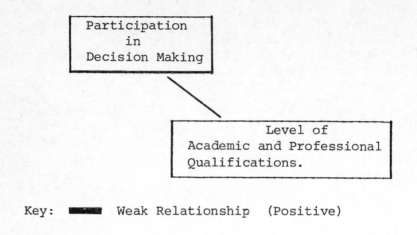

Key: ▆▆▆▆ Weak Relationship (Positive)

Figure 3.1   Participation in decision making (N = 603)

Is hierarchy of authority important?

Figure 3.2 shows highly significant and positive relationships between the index of hierarchy of authority and the index of job regulation and between the index of hierarchy of authority and the index of rule observation. These results indicate that the greater the emphasis on chain of command for work decisions, the greater the amount of rule observation and job regulation. The mean scores tend to support these correlations (Table 3.1). Mean score for hierarchy of authority is 2.87 (mean range across the nine departments, 2.62 to 3.14), is higher than for participation in decision making which is 1.47 (mean range across the nine departments, 1.25 to 1.79). The mean score of job regulation is 3.66 (mean range 2.59 to 3.91), indicating the respondents perceive these departments to be relatively formalised in their working procedures.

Further, a highly significant and positive association exists between the index of hierarchy of authority and the index or routineness of work. (Fig. 3.2.) This indicates that the respondents perceive that the more hierarchical the organisation the greater the degree of routineness of work. Organisations that are hierarchically oriented and more formal in procedure will require rules and regulations that involve substantial routine in daily work activities. In this way, senior management involved in making decisions concerning the overall department, can spend less time on decisions concerning daily work and still maintain control over personnel lower in the hierarchy. The mean score for

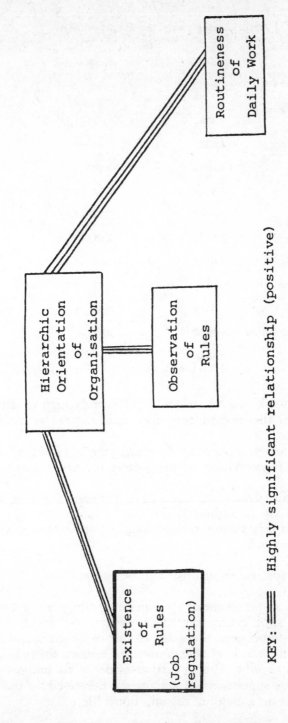

KEY: ≡ Highly significant relationship (positive)

Figure 3.2   Hierarchy of authority   (N = 603)

61

Table 3.1

Means and ranges across the nine departments
(N=603)

Structural properties	Mean score	Range across the 9 departments	Possible range
Participation in decision making	1.4782	1.43 − 1.79	1 − 5
Hierarchy of authority	2.8751	2.62 − 3.14	1 − 4
Job regulation	3.6672	2.59 − 3.91	1 − 4
Rule observation	2.4726	2.33 − 3.77	1 − 4
Rules manual	2.9768	2.73 − 3.51	1 − 4
Job descriptions	2.5426	1.81 − 3.18	1 − 4
Professional training	1.0746	1.04 − 1.49	0 − 5
Professional activities	.5274	0.39 − 1.28	0 − 3
Trade union activities	1.0033	0.78 − 1.31	0 − 3
Occupational specialisation	3.7788	2.65 − 4.11	0 − 6
Routineness of work	2.6838	2.59 − 3.87	1 − 4

routineness of work is 2.68, which is sufficiently high to support the conclusion that the respondents feel daily work activities to be routinely oriented.

The respondents perceive that the greater the hierarchy of authority, the greater the formalisation of procedures the more routine is daily work.

Because of the significant association between the observation of rules and hierarchy of authority, this can be interpreted as something more general, namely people feel themselves to be *closely supervised in doing their daily work.*

Relationship of the remaining organisational properties

Table 3.2 indicates that some of the remaining organisational properties are themselves significantly related. A positive and highly significant relationship exists between the index of rule observation and the index of job regulation, *indicating that those who observe the rules are those who also regulate jobs.* This is further evidence to support the conclusion that close supervision of activities is perceived by the respondents as an important activity of organisational life.

Table 3.2

Correlations between the three remaining structural properties (N=603)

Measures of formalisation, complexity and routineness	Job regulation	Rule observation	Presence of rules manual	Presence of job descriptions	Professional training	Professional activities	Trade union activity	Occupational specialisation	Routineness of work
Formalisation									
Job regulation	1.00	xxx	x	x	NS	NS	NS	NS	x
Rule observation		1.00	NS	NS	NS	NS	NS	NS	xxx
Presence of rules manual			1.00	x	NS	NS	NS	NS	NS
Presence of job descriptions				1.00	–xxx	NS	NS	NS	NS
Complexity									
Professional training					1.00	xxx	NS	NS	xxx
Professional activities						1.00	NS	NS	NS
Trade union activities							1.00	–xxx	NS
Occupational specialisation								1.00	NS
Routineness of work									1.00

Levels of significance

xxx	=	highly significant
xx	=	significant
x	=	moderately significant
NS	=	not significant

The index of professional training and the index of professional activities are highly significant and positively related, *implying that those with professional training undertake professional activities outside the department*. We have seen that those with higher educational qualifications and professional training tend to be promoted to managerial roles. Consequently, these are the people who tend to be involved in further professional development as opposed to the lower level social worker grades. Indeed, managerial adjustment to organisational and non-organisational demands has been widely discussed and documented, notably as early as Whyte (1956). He highlighted status as being an important factor in individual development. Those with status have more freedom to choose the sort of professional development they require. Those with status in SSDs are individuals higher in the managerial hierarchy, are well qualified and attend a greater number of professional meetings and conferences outside the organisation.

Interestingly, a negative and highly significant relationship exists between the index of trade union activity and the index of occupational specialisation. This relationship implies that with increasing occupational specialisation there is a reduction in trade union activity. As the respondents perceive these organisations as having a hierarchical structure accompanied by formality of procedure, it is likely that occupational specialisation will be geared toward departmental as opposed to professional (social work) division of labour. Mean score for occupational specialisation is relatively high at 3.78 (ranging from 2.65 to 4.1 across departments) and for trade union activity, the mean score is relatively low at 1.003 (ranging from 0.78 to 1.3). The mean scores tend to support this observation. The greater the increase of specialist activities, which we propose tend towards departmental as opposed to professional interests, the less attention is given to trade union activities.

A negative and highly significant relationship exists between the presence of job descriptions and the index of professional training. The relationship suggests that the greater the presence of job descriptions, the less the degree of professional training. We have suggested that those who are better qualified are those being promoted. Consequently, the respondents perceive job descriptions being utilised for those less well qualified, who are presumably lower down in the department. At the field work level, an individual social worker's job description may be written by his supervisor or area officer, or even managers at a higher level. Those in managerial positions may write their own job descriptions. What is significant is that those at field work level indicate that they are not in control of their job content and hence job description.

The index of routineness of work correlates positively with job regulation, with rule observation and with professional training. *The greater the routineness, the greater the degree of job regulation and rule observation.*

This supports previous findings, that with increasing emphasis on the hierarchy comes increasing formalisation of procedure and routineness of daily work. We have seen that both job regulation and rule observation are significantly related to hierarchy of authority, suggesting closeness of supervision. As routineness of work is significantly related to each of the three indices, it would seem that people perceive supervision to be a relatively routine activity. Further, the significant relationship between the index of routineness of work and the index of professional training, indicates the greater the routineness of work the greater the degree of professional training. Again, this adds to our previous conclusions that those better qualified are the ones promoted but their work, as much as for anyone else, is fairly routine in manner.

Does size of organisation affect the results?

Is size of organisation an important determinant of the results on organisation structure in this study? If size is taken to mean the total number of employees in an organisation, then the range in this study is broad, from just over 800 to 4,000 people. Being employed as one of 800 persons could be a different experience to being one of over 4,000. The problem is how should size be utilised in order to indicate differences between departments?

In this study, size is taken to represent a rank order of departments by the number of employees in the organisation. Size is statistically used as a control by partial correlation analysis.

As can be seen from Table 3.3, when size is used as a control in the relationship between hierarchy of authority and other structural properties, the relationships remain the same. The associations between hierarchy of authority and job regulation, rule observation and routineness of work are maintained in strength and direction. There is no change!

Where size of organisation was found to be a significant influence was over the number of job descriptions available and the number of persons sent for professional training. Basically, the larger the department, the greater number of job descriptions available for job holders and the greater the number of persons sent for professional training. Both findings are understandable. In a large organisation more well defined job descriptions would be a necessity so that people understand the limits of the work expected of them. This would not be so necessary in a smaller organisation as greater use would be made of interpersonal relationships between colleagues and supervisors.

Similarly, it is no surprise that larger departments have better quali-

Table 3.3

Hierarchy of authority and other structural properties when size of organisation
is controlled

(N=603)

Structural properties	Partical correlations with hierarchy of authority*
Participation in decision making	NS
Job regulation	XXX
Rule observation	XXX
Presence of rules manual	NS
Presence of job descriptions	NS
Professional training	NS
Professional activities	NS
Trade union activities	NS
Occupational specialisation	NS
Routineness of work	XXX

Levels of significance

XXX	—	highly significant
XX	—	significant
X	—	moderately significant
NS	—	not significant

* These are first order partial correlations, i.e., partial correlation co-efficients between each index listed and hierarchy of authority, controlling for size of organisation.

fied persons or can afford to send people on training courses to obtain professional qualifications. What is interesting from the results, is that the larger the organisations become, the less the perceived opportunity for the pursuit of activities with professional societies outside the employing organisation.

It is significant that size is not related, nor when used as control influences hierarchy of authority, job regulation, rule observation and routineness of work. *The respondents perceive that differences of size do not influence the hierarchic orientation of these departments or the routineness of work, but rather the degree to which day-to-day work is controlled.* Size seems to affect the volume of rules manuals in operation, job descriptions, those professionally trained and involvement in differing professional activities. Yet these factors seem to have little overall effect on the degree of centralisation and formalisation.

Summary

1 SSDs are seen by the respondents as centralised in terms of decision making over organisational policies.
2 Daily work is seen as restricted by rules and procedures leading to a feeling of routineness of work flow.
3 Supervisors are heavily involved in the work decisions of field work staff, either by,
    a) influencing work decisions to the extent that they are laying down rules for their subordinates, or
    b) overseeing subordinates closely, but following rules established by others, presumably senior managers.

In this way hierarchically oriented departments are able to control activities within the organisation through high supervisory involvement.

4 The respondents indicate that the way the organisations are established has little to do with their professional training and professional interests.

Study of culture at the organisation level[1]

Based on the results of the interviews from the first stage, two dimensions of culture at the organisation level were considered relevant,

1 The degree of challenge and responsibility that one could pursue in the organisation. Two indicators were drafted to represent challenge and responsibility; the index of *job autonomy* and the index of *career fulfilment* (Appendix 2).
2 The degree of conflict. Phrases such as 'fighting each other'; 'everybody is just as bad as everyone else'; 'just cannot get on with him or her, or them in general'; and words as 'backbiting', 'sneaky', 'untrustworthy' and 'troublesome' often appeared on the transcribed scripts. In an attempt to capture the themes that emerged from the interviews, two separate groups of questions were drafted, the index of *questioning authority* and the index of *interpersonal aggression*. (Appendix 2).

---

1   See Appendix 2 for the items on Organisation Culture.

From the original transmitted interviews, it became obvious that the respondents considered the structure of their departments, as the key influence to some of the problems they were facing. Hence, a cross-correlational analysis (using beta weights) was undertaken between aspects of organisation structure and the two dimensions of organisation culture. A large amount of data was gathered for this particular part of the study. The greater part of the data is not presented in this book, but in its place are diagrammatic summaries identifying the major trends. The summary for the studies of culture at both the organisation and group level are provided at the end of the section 'Study of culture at the group level', see p. 82.

Relationship between structure and culture

Figure 3.3 indicates the relationship between hierarchy of authority and the various aspects of organisation culture. Hierarchy of authority correlates strongly and negatively with job autonomy and career fulfillment. Hierarchy of authority only correlates strongly and positively with interpersonal aggression. *The respondents indicate that the more hierarchically oriented these organisations, the less the degree of job autonomy an individual is likely to experience.* Equally, the less fulfilling his career, the less people are likely to question authority. The positive correlation between hierarchy of authority and interpersonal aggression indicates that *the more hierarchically oriented these organisations, the greater the degree of interpersonal aggression amongst superiors, subordinates and colleagues.*

Figure 3.4 indicates that when relating measures of formality of procedures (i.e. rules and regulations) to aspects of organisation culture, certain relationships emerge. A moderate but negative relationship occurs between formality of procedure and job autonomy. A moderately strong and positive relationship emerges between formality of procedures and career fulfillment. A strong relationship occurs between formality of procedure and interpersonal aggression. *The results indicate that the greater the number of perceived rules and regulations, the less the feeling of having autonomy over one's job.* In contrast, *the greater the formality of procedure, the greater the sense of career fulfillment and the greater the sense of interpersonal aggression between superiors, subordinates and colleagues.*

The results are interesting. It is understandable that in hierarchically oriented organisations people feel that the degree of autonomy in their job, the ability to fulfill their careers and to question authority are substantially reduced. Figure 3.4 indicates that although feelings towards job autonomy are negatively oriented, career fulfillment is positively correlated to formality of procedures. This would seem to contradict the results in Figure 3.3, for career satisfaction is reduced

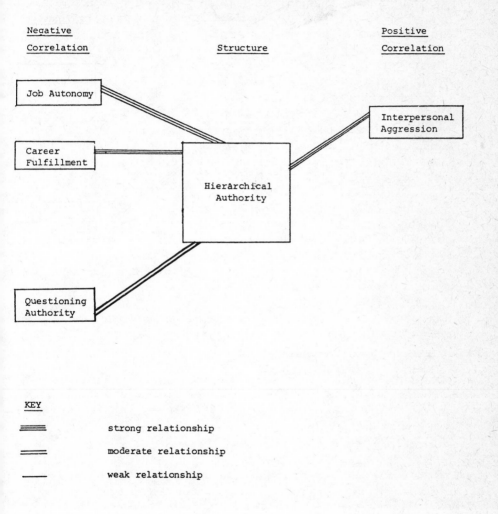

Figure 3.3   Relationship between hierarchy of authority
and organisation culture (N=603)

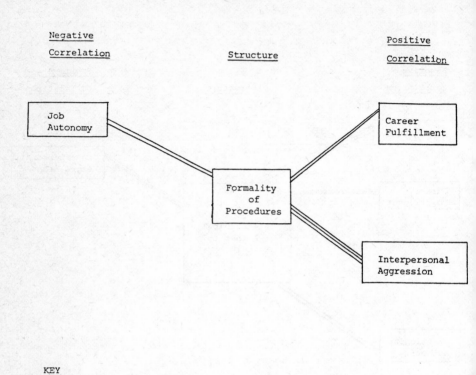

Figure 3.4   Relationships between formality of procedure
and organisation culture (N=603)

when relating it with the perceived hierarchical structure of the organisation but is increased when relating it to the formality of procedures.

Drawing on the results from the 'Study of organisation structure in the nine SSDs', p. 67, it was shown that supervisors are a key feature of the structure of the organisation. Supervisors not only provide a quality control service of the tasks undertaken by social workers, but further have to maintain and enforce the authority pattern of the organisation. Consequently, Figure 3.3 indicates that supervision is not viewed as a positive experience but more as something that reduces job satisfaction and career development. In contrast, having to meet the requirements of individual job descriptions and additional rules and regulation is seen as positive for career satisfaction, as no supervisors are involved.

Presumably, the respondents feel that career patterns have become relatively formalised. People realise what steps they have to go through to develop a career in the social services. Career development is likely to involve leaving aside professional casework skills when entering into the administrative hierarchy. Possibly, understanding that there are certain steps to follow to determine promotion, such as showing experience with certain types of professional social work, administration and supervision, induces a feeling of not being able to satisfy one's professional aspirations, but a career in line management is a good alternative even though it may seem restrictive.

Let us develop the argument further by examining figure 3.5 which indicates strong and positive relationships between complexity of relations, job autonomy and interpersonal aggression.

The more complex relationships become in an organisation, the greater the opportunity to develop autonomy in a small part of the total organisation. People have opportunities for professional training and by specialising, can control units within the organisation. Over time, people within units identify with their small group to the exclusion of other units, groups or departments. Hence, the larger any organisation becomes, the greater the diversity and the poorer the relationships, that are likely to develop.

Study of culture at the group level[1]

From the original unstructured interviews, we noticed that different groups within SSDs offered quite different points of view over the question of the degree of support they expected from superiors, sub-

---

1 See Appendix 2 for the items on Group Culture.

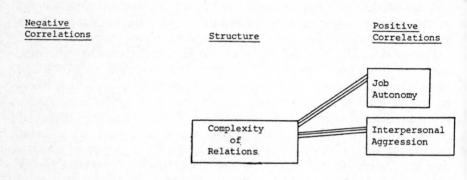

Negative
Correlations

Structure

Positive
Correlations

```
┌─────────────┐
│ Job         │
│ Autonomy    │
└─────────────┘
┌─────────────┐        ┌──────────────┐
│ Complexity  │        │ Interpersonal│
│ of          │        │ Aggression   │
│ Relations.  │        └──────────────┘
└─────────────┘
```

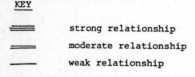

KEY

≡≡≡   strong relationship
≡≡   moderate relationship
───   weak relationship

Figure 3.5   Relationship between complexity of relations
and organisation culture (N=603)

ordinates and colleagues, concerning particular actions or decisions they made. Basically, there seemed to be little agreement over who should support who, over what actions and what decisions. Middle and senior managers in SSDs found it difficult to understand why social workers could not appreciate their constraints and hence the decisions they finally made. It is reasonably accurate to state that managers viewed social workers as unappreciative and unrealistic in their demands and work behaviour. Equally, the majority of social workers interviewed held negative feelings in terms of warmth and support towards colleagues, superiors and clients.

A social worker (county council)

I happened to undertake psychiatric social work training and one of the points emphasised on that course was warmth, support and understanding towards clients. Well, I can assure you that is not how I feel about most of my colleagues, I do not get much support within the department to do what I want and have learnt that I have to stand on my own two feet. Quite frankly, the same applies to clients because at the end of the day, I have a job to do and other clients to see to as well.

A minority however, felt positive towards their peers and superiors.

A social worker (metropolitan district)

I am really fortunate to work with people, whether my colleagues or boss, that are friendly and helpful and support me in difficult situations.

Because of the range of responses that were offered, it was decided to adopt questions that tested whether the climate surrounding people's jobs was supportive or constraining. This battery of questions came to be known as the job climate index (Appendix 2). The results are again presented in diagrammatic form, based on data gathered separately from managers, supervisors and social workers in nine SSDs.

Manager level perceptions of culture

Three interesting correlations arise when relating the managers' job climate index (JCI) to the other measures of culture and structure. Fig. 3.6 shows that the JCI has a highly significant and positive correlation with the index of career fulfillment and the index of complexity of relations but a negative and moderately significant correlation with the index of interpersonal aggression.

This suggests that the managers perceive that *the greater the sense of fulfillment in their career, the greater the sense of support in their job.*

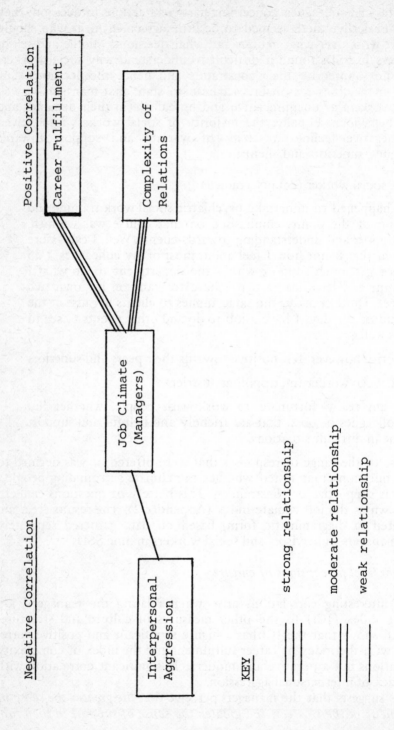

Figure 3.6   Job climate — managers (N=103)

74

Equally, *the more complex an organisation becomes, the greater the perceived importance of the managers.* However, the greater the degree of interpersonal aggression, the less the feeling of support in one's job.

The correlations between career fulfillment, complexity of relationships and job climate indicates a positive feeling towards developing careers in present day SSDs. The adjustments managers make to the demands of their organisation have long been documented. As indicated previously, Whyte (1956) stated that a satisfying part of managerial work is the acquisition of status. Status is an important factor in adjusting to meet organisational demands, for status introduces the incumbent to the concept of choice. The freedom to choose amongst alternatives is a positive motivating stimulus. Bonjean and Grimes (1970), report similar results stating that managers have better developed means of coping with formalisation than workers. Their higher standard of educational attainment, social status and income provide them with a better rationale and more opportunities to experience feelings of integration both on and off the job. However the correlation between interpersonal aggression and the JCI indicates that the managers as a group are aware of the tensions in their respective departments and are not so divorced from reality, as was supposed by some social workers in interviews.

Supervisor level perceptions of culture

Figure 3.7 indicates a highly significant and positive relationship between the JCI and the index of career fulfillment, but negative and strong relationships between hierarchy of authority and complexity of relationships and the JCI.

The positive relationship indicates that supervisors perceive *the greater the sense of fulfillment in their career, the greater the sense of support in their job.* This would seem to be self-fulfilling, in that those supervisors who feel their career to be developing positively would naturally feel a greater sense of support than constraint in their jobs. Possibly, supervisors view themselves as being on the 'first step' in the management career hierarchy and hence hold strong expectations for the future.

In contrast, the supervisory group perceive the hierarchical and complex relationships in SSDs as constraining. Supervisors have to manage teams of professional social workers in their casework duties and in addition, manage the rules, regulations and procedures instituted by the department. Having to operate within a dual role, means that two different types of demands are made upon supervisors. The demands are those of professional caseworkers and the requirements of administration. In the management literature, it is generally considered

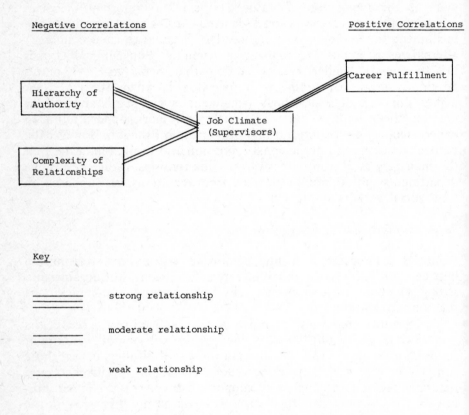

Figure 3.7   Job climate — supervisors (N=74)

76

that these two forces are incompatable. Hence, the greater the hierarchy and complexity of relationships, the greater the strain on the supervisors.

Social worker perceptions of culture

Figure 3.8 indicates a highly significant and positive association between the JCI and the index of career fulfillment. Negative and strong correlations exist between the index of questioning authority, the index of hierarchy of authority, the index of formality of procedures and the JCI. Social workers perceive *that the greater the sense of fulfillment in their career, the greater the sense of support in their job*. Equally, *the greater hierarchy of authority, the greater the formality of procedures and the greater the questioning of authority, the greater the degree of constraint social workers will experience in their daily work.*

The results are, at first glance, contradictory. How is it possible to obtain satisfaction from one's career, when key aspects of the organisation structure (i.e. the hierarchy and formality of procedures) are viewed as inhibiting and constraining? However, even in the 1950s, writers such as Brayfield and Crockett (1957) and March and Simon (1958) suggested that satisfaction and performance can serve as two independent variables. The fact that significant negative associations between the JCI and hierarchy of authority, formality of procedure and questioning authority are reported, does not mean to say that the prospect of a career in the social services is unattractive. Greater involvement with the hierarchy of the department may well lead to feelings of dissatisfaction, but the prospect of a career in the hierarchy of the social services is desirable, for it can bring benefits in terms of status and sense of power.

The respondents indicate that the only way to develop oneself is to be promoted up the hierarchy. Having to work with the frustration of operating at the lower end of the organisation was a pertinent issue in the open-ended interviews. In conversation with social workers, most stated that they were the only alienated group within SSDs. They realised that to question authority and the manner of decision making too much, may lead to substantial anxiety and aggravation for all concerned. Should however, a social worker question one or more decisions, then usually support from colleagues was forthcoming.

One strong theme is maintained in the responses of the three groups and that is the highly significant and positive relationship between job climate and career fulfillment. The three groups indicate that fulfillment in one's career is positive and supportive when looked at from the particular point of view of one's job. The high mean scores in Table 3.4 support the conclusion reached, that a career in the social services is seen in a positive light.

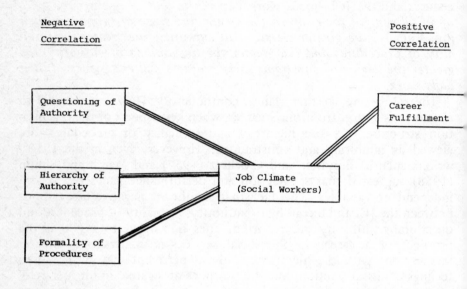

Negative
Correlation

Positive
Correlation

Questioning of
Authority

Hierarchy of
Authority

Formality of
Procedures

Job Climate
(Social Workers)

Career
Fulfillment

Figure 3.8   Job climate — social workers (N=426)

Table 3.4

Mean scores for the job climate index (JCI)

	Mean score	Range across departments	Possible range	Number of respondents
Managers' job climate index	3.43	2.98 − 3.96	1 − 5	103
Supervisors' job climate index	3.27	2.93 − 3.74	1 − 5	74
Social workers' job climate index	3.54	3.16 − 3.18	1 − 5	426

Organisational identity[1]

Four groups agreed to complete the team performance rating index; social workers, senior school workers, academics and engineers. Responses from the academic and engineers are used for purposes of comparison. The index required the respondents to first rank eleven characteristics of team performance in order from 1 to 11, with 1 representing the most important characteristic and 11, the least important. Second, attempt to identify on a scale 1 to 4 how the respondent's particular team may compare with an imagined overall departmental average (see Table 3.5 for the 11 characteristics).

Social workers Table 3.5 indicates the response of the social work group. The three most important characteristics identified by the social work group are *quality of work, harmony amongst team members and support of the team in emergencies.*

The three *least important* qualities identified are, *order and system, support of the department in emergencies and loyalty to the department.* In terms of average rating scores, the social workers rated their team high in relation to an imagined departmental average on the three characteristics they ranked highest. Equally, they offered low average rating scores on the three characteristics they ranked lowest.

Consequently, matters concerning the quality of one's work and functioning within teams are recognised as important aspects concerning working life. The three characteristics are also perceived as being high in terms of quality of performance with the rest of the department as shown in the average rating scores. The respondents indicate that not

---

1   See Appendix 2 for the Team Performance Rating Index.

Table 3.5

Social work group (N=63)

Average Rank order	Characteristics of team	Average rating score
(1)	Quality of work	3.75
(4)	Volume of work produced	3.25
(9)	Order and System	1.75
(5)	Enthusiastic effort	2.85
(7)	Persistence against obstacles	2.6
(11)	Loyalty to the department	1.52
(2)	Harmony amongst team members	3.52
(6)	Freedom of members to act on own judgement	2.7
(10)	Support of the department in emergencies	1.81
(3)	Support of the team in emergencies	3.15
(8)	Co-operation with other teams	2.12

only do they rank these characteristics as important but also hold a positive attitude towards them.

Senior social workers The responses of the senior social work group are similar to those of the social workers. Table 3.6 indicates that the three characteristics of *quality of work, support of the team in emergencies, and harmony amongst team members*, are ranked highest. The three characteristics ranked lowest are co-operation with other teams, order and system, and loyalty to the department. Similar to the social work group, those characteristics recognised as being important are rated high in relation to an imagined departmental average, whilst the three marked lowest, are rated below average.

Comparative ratings with academics and engineers For the purpose of comparison, two sample respondents were taken from academics in a Business School and engineers who worked on large capital projects in developing countries. An important feature of these two groups is that working in teams is considered vital, as tasks are distributed according to the teams available as opposed to being distributed to just particular

Table 3.6

Senior social work group (N=34)

Average rank order	Characteristics of team	Average rating score
(1)	Quality of work	3.45
(5)	Volume of work produced	3.15
(10)	Order and System	7.68
(4)	Enthusiastic effort	3.16
(6)	Persistence against obstacles	3
(11)	Loyalty to the department	1.26
(3)	Harmony amongst team members	3.09
(7)	Freedom of members to act on own judgement	2.84
(8)	Support of department in emergencies	2.04
(2)	Support of team in emergencies	3.36
(9)	Co-operation with other teams	1.96

individuals. By identifying similarities or differences between social services personnel and persons from other occupations, we can see to what extent social service personnel are different from others in different occupations.

The three characteristics considered important by the academic group were *enthusiastic, effort, quality of work and volume of work produced*. The three least important characteristics were *loyalty to the department, order and system and co-operation with other teams*. Academics in comparison to social work and senior social work staff are more concerned with individual effort and the quality and amount of work produced, rather than team spirit. In terms of co-operating with other teams, loyalty to the department and order and system, academics and social work staff rank these characteristics as being least important.

Similar to social work staff, academics give a high average rating score to those characteristics that are ranked high, and a low average rating score to those characteristics ranked low.

The engineers group offer broadly similar responses to those of the social workers and senior social workers. The three characteristics ranked highest are *harmony amongst team members, freedom of members to act on their own judgement and volume of work produced.* Engineers rank team harmony as important but also require a certain amount of freedom to act on their judgement. However, unlike the social workers and senior social workers, volume of work produced as opposed to quality of work is given a high ranking. The three characteristics ranked low are *loyalty to the department, support of the department in emergencies and co-operation with other teams.* Apart from the characteristics of order and system, the same low rankings are offered by the engineers for loyalty to the department and support of the department, as the social worker and senior social worker group.

Not only do the four groups of senior social workers, social workers, academics and engineers display similar scores in terms of ranking and average rating scores, but further, in terms of the relationship between the average rating score and the rank. Those team characteristics that are ranked high are awarded a rating score that is high on the scale. Those characteristics ranked low are awarded a low score on the scale. These comparative results give some indication as to the extent people are motivated to do the task. For all four groups, those characteristics ranked high seem also to be accompanied by positive attitude.

Summary

Figure 3.9 summarises the responses on organisation and group culture.

1 The degree of challenge and responsibility in the current organisations is perceived by the respondents as being low except for those promoted to managerial posts.

2 The degree of conflict in current organisations is felt to be high especially at the interpersonal level. The freedom and ability to question decisions is identified as being restrictive.

3 For warmth and support, the respondents in the three groups view some aspects of the hierarchic, formalised, and routine orientation of these organisation as a constraint.

4 Common to the three groups is the highly significant and positive correlation between the JCI, and the index of career fulfillment, indicating a positive attitude to career development.

5 In terms of organisational identity, the social workers and senior social workers note this dimension as low on their list of priorities. Identity with one's team is ranked as high on the offered characteristics of team functioning. Two additional groups of business school academics and engineers display similar results indicating low organisational identity and high team identity. Further, the emphasis on quality of work for both the social worker and senior social worker groups is high.

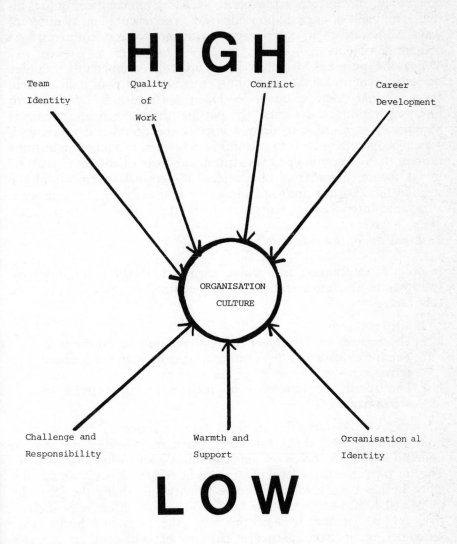

Figure 3.9   Summary of responses on organisation culture
(at organisation and group level)

83

Study of culture at the individual level

How does a person learn how to do his job, whilst on the job? We commonly call this process 'experience'. Every human being utilises his own data bank of mental knowledge (i.e. experience) in many different ways. Some use their experience towards their betterment and others to their detriment.

For the purposes of research, in order to competently examine personal accounts of the aspirations, fears and failures of individuals in their working life, we have developed a framework by which to interpret various statements. By putting these personal statements together, it is possible to draw a map of the norms and values with which people identify (i.e. culture) and further, examine the learning process that determines peoples attitudes and work behaviour, now and in the future. In order to obtain realistic personal statements of the relationship between one's self and work, we asked individuals (in semi-structured interviews) questions about the tasks they had to perform.

Task analysis at the individual level

In order to understand how people learn to do their job, it is necessary to isolate those factors that influence performance. Basically, there are four factors:

1 The task itself.
2 The feelings an individual holds about how to do the task.
3 The individual's felt degree of achievement from doing actual activities.
4 The results or outcomes of such activities in terms of performance.

Hackman (1969) identifies these as four fundamental influences on how a person goes about his work. When an individual is about to undertake work, he holds certain basic ideas about what he should do. This, in turn affects the level of stimulus he feels to actually do the job. Once he has been involved in some activity (i.e. doing the job), the individual begins to understand how good or bad, effective or ineffective, is his performance. In this way the individual learns what outcomes result from particular patterns of behaviour and he also begins to find that he can change his outcomes by changing his behaviour. In this way, he is learning about the job whilst doing his job, i.e. he develops criteria to assess his own performance and that of others.

In order to analyse how a person learns to do certain tasks the following factors are important, (see Figure 3.10).

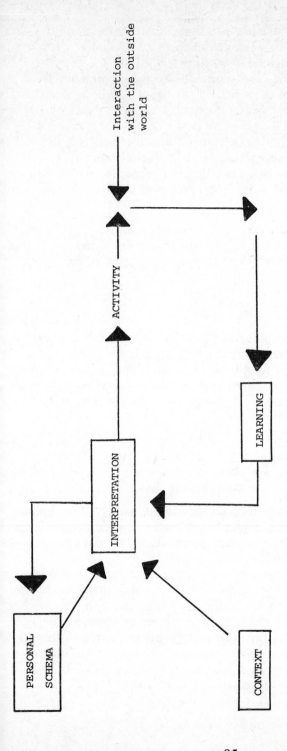

Figure 3.10 Task doing and task learning*

* The above model was developed after discussions with a colleague, Peter Russell, at the Cranfield School of Management, also with the help of my wife, Patricia Kakabadse

85

1 The ideas the individual has about different types of tasks; these ideas can be called personal schema.
2 The context from which he is working.
3 The personal schema and context strongly influence a person's felt stimulus to work and this leads to him making an interpretation on how a particular activity should be carried out.
4 The doing of the actual activity itself and the feedback the person receives from interacting with the outside world.
5 The degree of learning that the individual recognises which in turn will influence how he interprets similar tasks in the future.

The relationship between the task and the individual who is performing, is a dynamic one. It is a constantly changing and envolving process in which the individual builds up experiences which assist or hinder him, in doing his job.

Study of task processes in two SSDs[1]

Over 56 social service employees, ranging from social workers to directors of social work, were interviewed on a semi-structured basis. Each respondent was asked four basic questions. The responses ranged from simple yes/no answers to indepth accounts of what individuals had experienced, their present feelings and expectations. The four questions asked were:

1 What do you do in your job?
2 How do you feel about what you are doing?
3 What are you achieving by what you are doing?
4 What have you learnt from what you are doing?

Employees from particular contexts were chosen, namely those holding social work posts, those in senior social work positions, (i.e. team leaders or fieldwork supervisors); those in residential establishments and those in managerial positions above fieldwork supervisors.

Person to person interviews were conducted with respondents speaking into a tape recorder. The recording was transcribed by my secretary and sent back to the individual concerned for his or her clearance. Once the script had been cleared, we undertook a detailed content analysis of each script. The statements presented in the next sections are representative of the sentiments of the majority in interview. Further transcripts of interviews can be seen in Appendix 3. Most of the key issues emerging are presented in tabular form.

1 See Appendix 3 for additional transcripts of interviews.

Responses at social worker level

Case 1: social worker (Metropolitan District — professionally qualified and newly appointed to post)

> *What do you do in your job?*
> I prefer to undertake work with children and families. I find it difficult to relate to people who have mental health problems.
>
> *How do you feel about what you are doing?*
> I am not well organised . . . I don't feel that I have much experience. I feel I should be doing the job for a lifetime before I really know what it is all about. I suppose one is working all the time, but I seem to be concentrating more on the department than different clients.
>
> *What are you achieving by what you are doing?*
> I am beginning to understand what sort of clients get on well with me and me with them. I am also beginning to understand which colleagues I should approach to discuss what problem. I suppose I am learning how to work within a team.
>
> *What have you learned from what you are doing?*
> I find this 'cover yourself, cover yourself, cover your department' thing a nuisance because you get where you cannot make a proper decision. Covering yourself can inhibit what you decide on. I find it quite difficult to know when my ideas or my feelings are in conflict with the departments or when me as a representative of the department rather than as an individual has to take action.

Case 2: hospital social worker (professionally qualified with many years experience).

> *What do you do in your job?*
> I think we probably have a lot more forms to fill in. We have to be more strict in filling them in than before in the Health Services.
>
> *How do you feel about what you are doing?*
> I used to think that a lot of the work of the hospital social services was acting as a sort of clearing house, passing problems on to somebody else to deal with. But, I think now, that whether it is a result of being part of a bigger organisation. I think there is a great deal more done by hospital social

workers within the hospital and outside the hospital, than used to be done.

What are you achieving by what you are doing?
We receive a great number of referrals of elderly people who for one reason or another are immobile. This is not a particular good hospital for them to stay and so we have to get them transferred to one of the outlying hospitals. I found I have developed administrative skills in relating to social workers in other hospitals so that I am satisfied that the handover of the patient is smooth and efficient and the standard of care is as high as it would have been here.

What have you learnt from what you are doing?
What I have learnt are now my main strengths, and these are knowledge and experience. The knowledge I have is knowledge of how people function and a lot of that I gained from my social work course. My experience comes from having been employed as a social worker and where it is most useful is in giving me the knowledge of resources available and how to use them. Just because you are a social worker does not mean that all you have to know is something about psychology. You have to know what resources are required, how to get them and how to use them.

Social worker responses A fundamental theme of all the social worker responses is the importance of organisational issues in thinking about tasks. As can be seen in Figure 3.11 the majority of the respondents in this study displayed negative feelings over matters that are concerned with their respective departments. All the social workers felt restricted by the system of allocation of cases and by the amount of daily administration. One social worker responded consistently to all four questions by stating that he wished to become more community minded. He could just as easily have been entered as displaying a negative feeling (Figure 3.11), as the person was asked about a 'here and now' issues and instead decided to respond with a statement about a future objective. For him the question remains as to how he feels about the here and now.

Only the hospital social worker offered a positive response, by identifying that an increase in organisational size has led to greater personal responsibility.

In terms of personal achievement, the responses indicated that achievement is linked with one's career development in terms of the hierarchy of the department. Feelings tended to be both positive and negative, dependent on whether opportunities were available for career

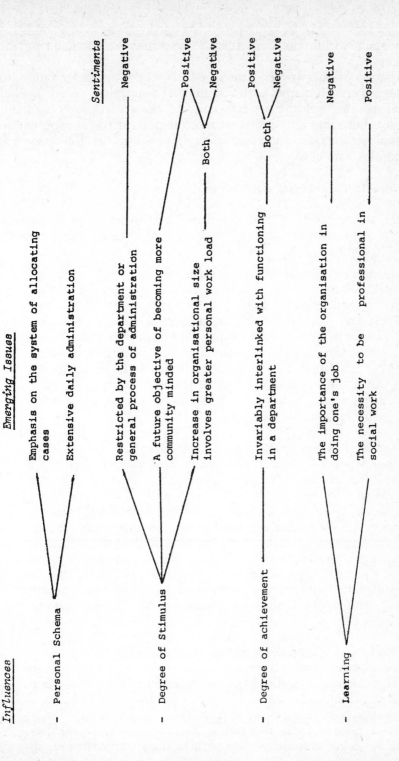

Figure 3.11   Tasks and sentiments of social workers

development within the departmental hierarchy or restricted by the hierarchy.

Only one social worker attempted to relate the organisation to professional involvement with clients. The hospital social worker summarised the majority of responses of the social workers in this study by indicating that it is first more important to function within the employing organisation and then if possible, develop long-term relationships with clients.

Responses at senior social worker level

Case 1: senior social worker (metropolital district — professionally qualified with substantial experience at senior social worker level).

What do you do in your job?
My job is to allocate and supervise the work of social workers, and to ensure the work is done properly. Allocation of the work is not difficult, but supervision can be difficult. There are always a lot of working parties in session attended by social workers. There are also a lot of meetings that I have to attend. Consequently, finding time to supervise social workers is difficult. If I have been available, the social worker is not. I think one of the biggest problems is trying to make yourself as available as possible while doing the other work you are supposed to be doing.

How do you feel about what you are doing?
As a supervisor, I am still learning. Sometimes, I feel that I tend to be too superficial, possibly because of my own inadequacies and my own fears and possibly because of my position as a first line manager, I don't delve deeply enough into cases with social workers, partly, because there are half a dozen people coming to see me with all their most difficult problems and I feel like saying 'Oh, shut up!, I can only deal with one thing at a time'. Over the past year, I have come to terms with this more by not being at social workers beck and call. The biggest bind is paperwork and that tends to get left to one side.

What are you achieving by what you are doing?
I hope I am helping to provide as good a service as possible to meet the needs of the client, whatever particular client group they belong to. I would like to see us providing more community oriented services so that groups such as the elderly can remain in the community as long as possible. I would like to see more preventive work with families, but in the present

climate, I do not think we do this sort of work, and I think this is reflected by the number of children we have in care. Of course, all this is time consuming and what is worse, more and more work is being placed on us. However, I think a lot of the problems could be helped by the management team and by the way they allocate resources and deal with counsellors and committees. I think as far as that is concerned, they are quite weak.

What have you learnt from what you are doing?
I try to interfere too much with social workers instead of having a policy of 'OK you get on with it', and allowing different people of having slightly different ways of working. Part of the problem is that there are pressures on me to gather certain types of information and pass it on. I think both ourselves as seniors and social workers themselves have to be aware of the problems we jointly face over recording, doing and filling in forms. There needs to be a certain amount of flexibility over administration.

Case 2: Consultant social worker (metropolitan district – professional, qualified with many years experience in social work and now specialising in mental health work).

What do you do in your job?
What I don't do is meet clients, or at least, very seldom meet clients. I only meet them when they have a complaint about this particular area. What I do is work closely with the boss who gives me a job and I have to set the framework and work towards achieving those goals within a certain time. I am more of a manager than a social worker because in order to solve a problem I have to assess the resources available in relation to the goals I have set in the time available and review the progress being made from time to time.

How do you feel about what you are doing?
I think at times I am quite a big cog and at others quite a small cog. You have to be one or the other at different times. At the area directors meeting I am one of ten people. If I am involved with something in mental health, then I become *primus inter pares* within that group. Fundamentally, whether I can contribute a great deal or little to meetings, I now have more positive feelings about what I do than when I was a social worker.

What are you achieving by what you are doing?

I am making colleagues and subordinates more aware of mental health problems, how to recognise them and cope with them. Perhaps, just as important, I am setting up administrative systems to cover mental health work.

What have you learnt from what you are doing?
My greatest area of achievement is in my negotiations with other organisations, i.e. health services, police and voluntary organisations. Prior to Seebohm, individual social workers in whatever specialism tended naturally over time to develop contacts with other organisations as part of their daily work. The situation has now changed and having good working relationships with other organisations has become more of a management problem than just a social work problem. One should recognise it to be a management problem and not complain about not being able to contact other people.

Senior social worker response As can be seen in Figure 3.12 three themes dominated the discussions: the allocation of work to social workers; the supervision of that work; and the need to gain power to determine greater control over the use and allocation of resources.

Most senior social workers felt positive about the activities in which they were involved. Sentiments such as 'doing the right thing', 'developing other people', 'making sure the right task be given to the right person', were expressed. Certain senior social workers stated that they actively pursued power in order to gain greater control over the resources they required to do their work. The majority of the respondents felt that playing power games was justified as resources were scarce and further it seemed to be expected of seniors to be involved in such activities.

However, negative feelings were expressed over the need to be involved in daily administration. Administration was seen as something ranging from being tiresome but necessary, to something as unnecessary and a way of controlling others by senior management.

In response to the question on achievement, positive sentiments were expressed. Fostering good working relationships within teams and establishing systems of work that are understandable and relatively easy to utilise, was viewed as a priority. Some senior social workers stated they put substantial effort into working towards a community oriented service, emphasising the preventive nature of their work. Again, in order to determine ends in community work, the need to gain power was strongly emphasised.

Two themes emerged from the question what have senior social workers learnt to be the key skills in their job. These are delegation of responsibility and the development of interpersonal skills.

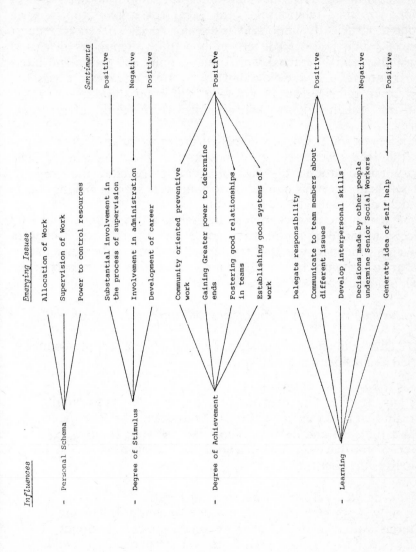

Figure 3.12   Tasks and sentiments of senior social workers

It was considered important by the seniors to delegate certain responsibilities to field workers and equally protect them from senior managers. Consequently, competence at delegation implies skills in interpersonal interaction. One cannot delegate without knowing how to engender trusting relationships. In fact, these two topics were considered sufficiently important for senior social workers to request guidance, training and feedback on how they themselves delegated responsibility and interacted with other people. Delegation and interpersonal interaction were linked with information flow. It was felt important to inform team members of the issues and decisions made by others, usually higher management, which could affect team performance.

Some senior social workers discussed their particular model of social work that they were trying to promote in their department. The majority talked around the idea of trying to generate the image of client self-help. Previous modes of working were seen as making clients dependent on individual social workers.

Some senior social workers felt themselves as being undermined by the decisions made by senior managers. The sentiments expressed were negative and the view was that the feeling of being undermined had to be learnt to live with. In fact, being undermined was seen as part of the overall 'political' game of being a manager.

Responses from officers in residential establishments

Case 1: Officer-in-charge, children's residential home (county council — qualified as a residential social worker).

> *What do you do in your job?*
> I am the officer-in-charge and my responsibility is to run the team that runs this home. I try to understand both the clients and the staff and not to differentiate between the two. But when you have an inexperienced staff, they need as much help as the clients.
>
> *How do you feel about what you are doing?*
> I allow both staff and clients a lot of leeway in coming to terms with themselves and the establishment. I suppose I make it difficult for myself because I am so readily available when they need me that sometimes I am unable to do anything else. I only wish I could switch off . . . when I suppose from anyone else's point of view, it would be better. My superior has often told me not to take responsibilities for everything on my shoulders. Well, it's not very good advice when a lot of people are depending on you, but I think that is also a weakness on my part.

What are you achieving by what you are doing?
I think there is too much emphasis placed on administration and not enough on people. Again I see my job as dealing with the people in my care and trying to help them come to terms with their situation. What makes things worse is that I have an extremely in-experienced staff and when I am here, I have to deal with everyone's problems. I just cannot find time to do this. The whole situation has become more bureaucratic and I am finding it hard to train my staff in residential social work and the administration of residential social work.

What have you learnt from what you are doing?
One thing I have learnt is that a major weakness lies in the hierarchy, who will not accept that the workers themselves are under terrific pressure and have their own problems in trying to help clients come to terms with their own problems. There is definitely a lack of communication between the hierarchical levels and I do not seem to be able to overcome that.

Case 2: Residential social worker (metropolitan district — qualified as a psychiatric nurse).

What do you do in your job?
I find myself more in management than dealing with clients and I really wanted a job that had greater client contact. I find myself looking after 14 part-time helpers, 3 domestics and 2 cooks.

How do you feel about what you are doing?
I do not feel very happy with what I am doing partly because social service organisations have too many bosses which makes the whole department too bureaucratic. I find it very difficult to get through to my immediate superior over small things which require him to give guidance or make a quick decision. I find that so much red-tape is involved that I eventually do not bother.

What are you achieving by what you are doing?
It is very difficult to know what I am achieving. I find myself torn between administering a home and looking after clients. I would like to be more knowledgeable about knowing clients as persons, knowing their relations and finding out as much as I can about them. I think I am relatively successful in getting the relatives of the clients involved as much as possible in the life and daily concerns of the client.

What have you learnt from what you are doing?
I see my main strength as really becoming annoyed when I cannot get involved or solve a problem. When I really want something done, I think I am strong enough to stir everyone up even to the point of annoying my superiors. I nearly always get things done. What I have learnt, is that if I kick up a fuss, I'm bound to lose somewhere else, or at a later date. One also has to be careful, in that if one is seen to be continually arguing, eventually you're ignored.

Case 3: Residential social worker (metropolitan district – professionally un-qualified but in residential social work for a number of years).

What do you do in your job?
I work with adolescents and adults. I see my role as being a rehabilitative worker. My ultimate aim is to return clients back to their families and also I suppose so that the client is sufficiently able to interact with field workers.

How do you feel about what you are doing?
I feel both bad and good. There is a lack of trained staff for residential social work and therefore we are given an inferior status to social workers and about that I do not feel too good. We should not be seen as being separate as we are working within the same area. On the other hand, the good thing about this work is that one has a captive audience in that you have removed clients from outside pressures and problems. One has the opportunity to work with clients intensively and, if sufficiently motivated, one can use the advantages of the total institution, which is often thought to be detrimental to the well being of the individual.

What are you achieving by what you are doing?
I make full use of the residential setting within which I work. I also enjoy my work.

What have you learned from what you are doing?
I have learned that there are a lot of skills in the present post-Seebohm departments. They have however, to be used more adequately. The problem is that the better qualified people are automatically seen as good management potential and eventually promoted. There is no way of developing your career on the case work side.

Residential officers responses Two basic themes dominate the answers to the 4 questions. As can be seen in Figure 3.13, the two themes

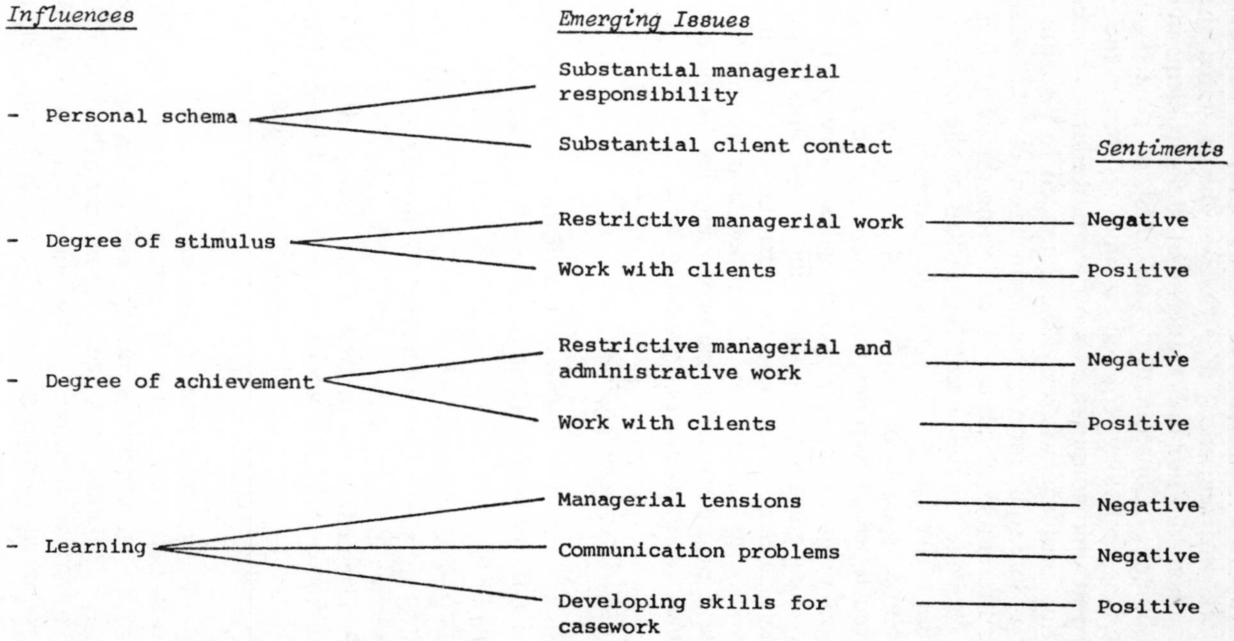

Influences

- Personal schema

- Degree of stimulus

- Degree of achievement

- Learning

Emerging Issues

Substantial managerial responsibility

Substantial client contact

Restrictive managerial work

Work with clients

Restrictive managerial and administrative work

Work with clients

Managerial tensions

Communication problems

Developing skills for casework

Sentiments

Negative

Positive

Negative

Positive

Negative

Negative

Positive

Figure 3.13   Tasks and sentiments of residential officers

are administrative work/managerial communication and developing skills for work with clients. The officers-in-charge stated that head office management did not fully understand their problems in residential establishments. Consequently, the officers tended to view administration as something required by superiors, but in their view as unnecessary and time consuming. Case 1 felt powerless to overcome his communication problem, whereas Case 2 tended to generate conflict situations to ensure some form of communication.

The two different strategies of either 'letting things happen to you' or 'fighting to make yourself heard' seemed to be the only two strategies that senior officers in residential homes had adopted.

The residential social worker's response of being virtually totally client oriented (Case 3), typifies the responses from other residential social workers. The majority of residential social workers saw their task as developing good client relationships for therapeutic work. Over organisational issues, the response was that of either no interest or simply ignorance as to the key departmental concerns. Sentiments expressed were positive towards casework and developing clients, but negative towards managerial and organisational matters.

Responses from the managerial group

Case 1: Assistant director (metropolitan district — not professionally qualified but a former senior administration officer in the pre-Seebohm welfare department).

What do you do in your job?
Basically, my job is, in two parts. To provide and deliver a social service in a geographic patch, and secondly, to be part of a management team to look at the delivery of service to parts of the district as a whole. In addition, I have a liaison role with the area health authority and a planning role with the area health authority.

How do you feel about what you are doing?
Very frustrated. For delivery of service, we are in a situation whereby social services generally are under tremendous attack from all sides. It is becoming increasingly difficult to deliver a service because of the general attitudes of the public, counsellors especially and some of the other helping services . . . Not only are we being pressed by increasing demands, but at the same time we are being restricted on resources.

As far as the planning aspects are concerned, particularly liaison with the area health authority, again it is becoming increasingly difficult and very frustrating in terms of long-term planning.

The future is so uncertain both for social services and area health.

There is a lack of decisiveness about the planning process which can be so long winded and involved. Various personalities come creeping into the planning process that it virtually becomes non-existant.

What are you achieving by what you are doing?
Now the situation, particularly in this industrial relations and economic climate, has become so difficult, that even the objective of holding together that which we have, is now probably an objective which I doubt we are going to be able to achieve. In terms of what we have achieved, I had better be frank — precious little. In terms of delivery of service to clients, I think we have achieved little, and in certain areas we have substantially gone back on achievements we had prior to re-organisation. I think we have managed to hold together a certain amount of staff morale, and that is about all I think I have achieved in terms of my own area involvement. In terms of joint planning . . . it has taken a lot of manipulating, where people now recognise what the problem is, and answers have to be got and either we will jointly plan or we won't. Whether it is an achievement or not, we have at least got all the chief officers to recognise that there is a problem which has to be answered . . . Also, the departmental management team finds itself increasingly restricted in its range of options, because we are so tied by centralised activities. The discussion at the DMT (departmental management team) tend almost to be administrative discussions and we seem to spend less time to really discuss the improvement of service delivery to clients.

What have you learnt from what you are doing?
I have learnt that local government has changed rapidly. The upsurge of militance amongst staff, the upsurge of militance in pressure groups, the upsurge of politics with a capital P, is something most of us have not experienced quite to the extent that it has got to now. Counsellors are a big problem as they seem to think of us as people with whom they should find fault. Also greater commitment is required from the chief officers management team for they not only seem to keep us in the dark about many issues but further, when we get together we just haggle and fight.

99

Case 2: Director (metropolitan district — professionally qualified with many years experience in social work).

What do you do in your job?
Basically, my job is to try and ensure that the overall objective of obtaining an appropriate service and having regard to community needs is attained. The methods I use to achieve this objective is on three fronts basically. One is to obtain resources for the department from the council and consequently . . . an awful lot of time is spent on relationships with members. This is a very sensitive area in that the attitudes I inherited . . . were negative ones and this has been shown in members discussions with me and to me personally.

Second, it is necessary to establish good relationships with other chief officers because of the influence of certain key chief officers especially the Treasurer.

The third area is the staff themselves and particularly the senior management staff within the Social Service department. A lot of time is spent on management meetings to ensure that the staff do the job they are paid to do . . . Again, one spends far more time in trying to manipulate people to help them to make decisions which are in the interest of the clients. This means a lot of backdoor work outside meetings; for example, if there is a dispute with the area manager of 'x' area it would necessitate me having meetings with each members of that team privately. Because they are fighting amongst themselves and cannot agree, as somebody from outside, I can get them to have a joint view.

How do you feel about what you are doing?
I feel that most of what I am doing is not bearing fruit, for a variety of reasons. First, this particular department is such . . . that it inhibits the development that one would have expected. For example, there were more facilities available in my last department than in this one. This department has few qualified social workers and this may have an influence on the actions and motivation of staff. The departmental management team comprises of X people, two of whom are not professionally qualified and they are assistant directors. Certainly, their thinking on how one would expect a professional to develop makes it very difficult to bring forward new developments in the actual areas where they are managers. Another problem area is the role of the chief executive and his department. His department is split into two divisions . . . X and Y, both of which seriously interfere

100

with the management of this department.

A simple example of the present industrial action is one where the members have made a decision as to what I shall do and therefore, I am not in control of the situation. In this context, they have been advised by both X and Y and in consequence, I am not free to act in the way I would have done. I simply feel frustrated in this sort of situation.

What are you achieving by what you are doing?
When I first arrived at the department, there were bad relationships with members and questionable relationships with staff for a variety of reasons. So coming into a rather difficult situation, there was scope to develop new patterns . . . in such things as staff relationships, member relationships etc. I feel I have achieved a more positive relationship with members. We are now in a position where they have agreed that social services should take priority over all other departments with regard to resources. With staff, I thought we were achieving something, until this present industrial action (*a strike was being threatened at the time*). I feel these achievements may now be somewhat limited, especially if the members react badly to the situation. However, I feel because of the general situation, there has been little improvement as far as clients are concerned.

What have you learnt from what you are doing?
From my previous experience and from this post, it came home to me that it wasn't merely a question of managing through instruction but rather managing through personal relationships. Consequently, when I came to this authority, I saw it as my job to build on staff relationships so as to develop staff relationships as far as possible. Management control means nothing unless you have good staff relationships and staff are prepared to work with you and for you. This extends to members of the committee, the management team and other organisations.

Social work managers responses As can be seen in Figure 3.14, the basic themes generated by the four questions are: developing good interpersonal relationships; liaising with other departments within the authority and outside organisations; manipulating the system; and managing grievances as they arise.

Fundamentally, social work management is seen less in terms of control and authority and more in terms of facilitation and working with people. The process of facilitating relationships with others on a

101

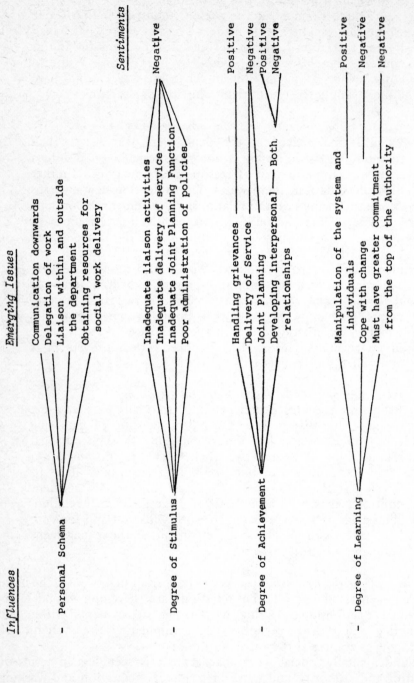

Figure 3.14   Tasks and sentiments of social service managers

more personal basis, was viewed positively. However, most managers expressed frustration, dismay and often feelings of not achieving objectives when involved in joint planning and liaison activities. Joint planning and liaison work involves long term negotiations and the outcome of protracted negotiations with others is unpredictable.

Managers recognised these feelings of frustration and blamed the unclear nature of managerial work as the prime cause. Numerous meetings have to be attended. Short and long term objectives are seen as constantly being changed through negotiation with substantial numbers of people. Hence, progress is viewed as agonisingly slow with the possible consequence that an individual's involvement in a particular project may go unrecognised. It takes time to complete a project and further because a number of people are involved, the contribution of one individual may not be appreciated or simply forgotten. Slow progress, ambiguity and frustration are recognised as normal everyday occurrences.

Summary

Figure 3.15 summarises the responses of the four groups of social workers, senior social workers, residential officers and social work managers.

1 Social workers, display negative feelings towards current systems of allocation of work and daily administration. They offer positive statements towards being professional in social work activities.

2 Senior social workers offer positive statements over such issues as the ability to gain power and control resources, develop a career in the social services and the ability to generate a positive team identity. Yet a number of senior social workers were suspicious that their role was being undermined by their superiors. Note that none of the managers in the sample identify themselves as undermining the role of the senior social worker. In fact, the problem in the eyes of managers was how to delegate further responsibility to senior social workers. In addition, senior social workers felt strongly that they should be promoting a stronger sense of professionalism amongst their team members.

3 Residential staff discussed two issues; the problem area of managerial work, and work with clients which is seen in a positive light.

4 Social work managers indicate that administering internal departmental policies, liaison activities, and joint planning

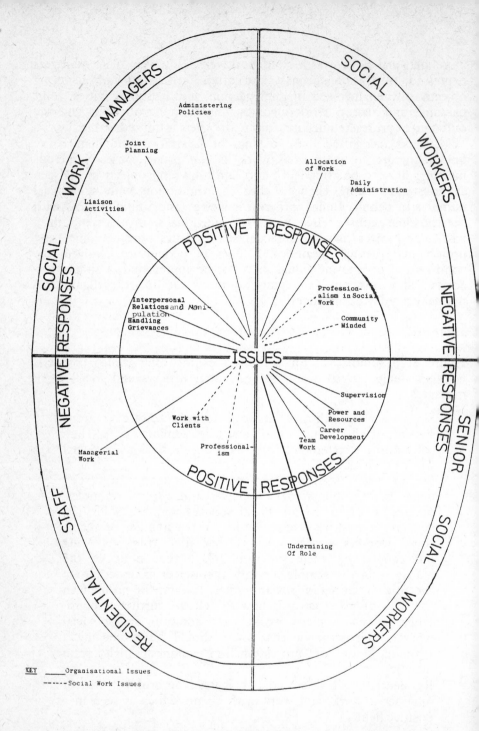

Figure 3.15 Summary of the responses of four groups on issues concerning tasks

functions with outside bodies, requires substantial improvement. Handling personal and group grievances and developing and promoting interpersonal relationships is worthwhile and produces positive results.

Mix of cultures

Discussion of the research findings is presented as follows: cultural norms and values in SSDs; career development; and what is being learnt?

Cultural norms and values in SSDs

Norms and values are the key to any discussion on culture, as norms and values are central to understanding individual and group behaviour. How does an individual decide what is appropriate behaviour? If an individual decides that a particular form of action is required on his part then that indicates certain feelings the person holds of how things ought to be. Such an expression of feelings can be termed a personal value and if further developed into behaviour becomes normative (i.e. a commonly held norm). Two psychologists Katz and Kahn (1966) suggest that organisations are social systems compiled of multiple sets of role behaviour. Norms serve as prescriptions of behaviour and values are the ideological justification for that behaviour. In this way, an organisation can focus on one or more common purposes. The concept of one or more common purposes makes sense. Individual social workers may be given the scope to generally agree with the overall social work purpose of their employing organisation and yet allowed the freedom to determine their sub-goals in terms of individual task activities. Work with children for example, involves organising adoptions, developing professional relationships with different members of the family, visiting private foster homes and supervising children in care. In doing such tasks, the objectives of the organisation are met and social workers may equally have freedom to develop their own style of working with clients in the field.

The freedom to develop multiple goals is not just a complementary process for it can and often does, lead to conflict. The conflict could centre at the individual level over particular cases where different personal values would motivate single persons to reach a different decision to their colleagues.

Equally, the conflict could be at the organisational level. For example, police organisations and SSD's have never had a comfortable relationship. Both sides have never been able to trust the 'true' intentions of the other, even though individuals in both groups have to

105

act as caseworkers and law enforcers in different circumstances. Their differences in personal values and norms of accepted behaviour have made it virtually impossible for them to co-operate.

Consequently, what norms and values emerge from the research studies described in this chapter? Turning to the discussion on cultures in chapter 1, the predominant characteristics of working within a task oriented culture are, the task or problem at hand, skills and expertise, working within team settings and low identity with the total organisation. The predominant characteristics of a role culture are emphasis on rules and procedures, definitions of authority relationships, formal procedures for communication and an organised and controlled career path for individuals. The key features of a power culture are controlling and influencing the activities of others, obtaining resources, strategic negotiations and maintaining control. Table 3.8 summarises the major characteristics identified in the research that fall under the categories of role, task and power cultures.

The characteristics identified that are supportive towards a task culture are team identity, emphasis on quality of work, support of one's team in emergencies. The negatively oriented characteristics working against a task culture are the poor relationships between superiors and subordinates, a low emphasis on challenge and responsibility, low perceived job autonomy and little perceived questioning of authority.

The characteristics in favour of a role culture are the establishment of hierarchical authority relationships, formality of procedures, hierarchic career development and a management that is favourably inclined towards complex organisational relationships. The characteristics that are negatively oriented towards a role culture are a low identity with the total organisation and little support, especially from the lower ranks of the organisation, for the current order and system.

Not only social services personnel but engineers and academics seem to display similar characteristics. They indicate that in doing their tasks, they prefer to operate in a task oriented culture. Most academics and engineers are employed by large organisations and thereby have to face certain organisational constraints. The constraints are not simply ones of having to cope with additional administration but those of having to work within two different value systems. For example, most of the engineers interviewed stated that the greater part of their work is conducted abroad, within small team settings. The preparation of reports on large engineering projects is important, for the reports have to indicate in detail the plan of the total project. On return to the company, reports and 'scopes of work' are taken from the engineer and possibly offered to other engineers. The original engineer working on the project report would not be informed about any decisions made on his report. The lack of opportunity to finish a job and develop

Table 3.7

Cultural characteristics in 12 SSDs

Task culture	Role culture	Power culture
Positive characteristics	Positive characteristics	Positive characteristics
Team identity Emphasis on quality of work Supporting the team in emergencies	Hierarchy of authority Hierarchic career development Positive management attitude to complex organisational relationships	Good facilitation of inter-personal relations Managing grievances Manipulation of resources and people towards strategic ends
Negative characteristics	Negative characteristics	Negative characteristics
Poor relationships between superiors and subordinates Low emphasis on challenge and responsibility Low job autonomy Low questioning of authority	Low identity with organisation Little support for order and system	Liaison with other departments and organisation is poor Joint planning is poor Administering policies is poor Coping with change is difficult Obtaining greater commitment from other chief officers and chief executive is difficult

individual professional interests were the key factors for the poor relationships between professional engineers and the senior executives within their employing company.

Many of the social workers interviewed complained of similar frustrations. Lack of information about projects or other programmes in the organisation and a general feeling of not knowing what is happening in the organisation, serve to generate feelings of animosity towards management. Hence, although team identity is high and social workers place emphasis on their quality of work, poor relationships are seen to exist between superiors and subordinates with little autonomy and challenge in individual jobs. Two conflicting sets of norms are in operation.

The results in the 'Study of organisation structure in nine SSDs', (p 67), identify the importance of supervisory activity. It seems therefore, that the two cultures 'meet' at the supervisory level. The senior social worker group are faced with the responsibility of having to manage two seemingly irreconcilable demands. A senior social worker stated in interview:

Supervision can be done in two ways. Some senior social

107

workers never stir outside their office unless in an emergency. Myself, I make time available so that all that are on my social workers' caseload, I know personally. You see, I think that most of my colleagues fall into the former category, and after a while they end up supervising the departments rules and regulations.

Those undertaking supervisory activity (senior social workers, team leaders) occupy the *first order gatekeeper* line for the service they provide is reconciling the demands of two different sets of norms. (Figure 3.16). Task norms concerning client welfare have to be reconciled with organisational norms of maintaining the role hierarchy. Senior social workers are likely to spend a large proportion of their time ensuring that social workers complete their administrative tasks, for they in turn will have to face the demands of the next level of management. These findings support the conclusions that Parsloe and Stephenson (1978) reached, that senior social workers have a high administrative content in their workload.

Equally, a great deal of time will be spent by senior social workers in group meetings discussing developments within the hierarchy. The amount of time spent discussing casework issues is not high in comparison. In fact, attending meetings has been identified in these studies as the principal activity of senior social workers.

From the interviews in the 'Study of culture at the individual level', (p 103), the responses of some of the senior social workers indicate that the demands of both cultures seem to be within their control. Facilitating relationships within teams and acquiring resources for the team (aspects of a task culture) are seen in an equally positive light with personal career development and the more bureaucratic demands of supervision. Yet an expressed fear was that their role could be undermined. An often expressed anxiety of persons operating in a role culture is the fear of loss of legitimate control. Although some senior social workers indicated that they were able to manage conflicting demands, others expressed that they experienced stress. The 'gate keepers' are the persons at risk within organisations, in terms of personal stress and anxiety.

For the senior management group, the common link between the positive responses such as the facilitation of interpersonal relationships, managing grievances, and the negative responses such as liaising, joint planning, administering policies, coping with change and obtaining greater commitment from the top, is that these activities involve developing relationships with large numbers of individuals and groups. Working with others towards obtaining resources, allocating resources, controlling and influencing the activities of others is symptomatic of persons whose primary objective is strategic development from a

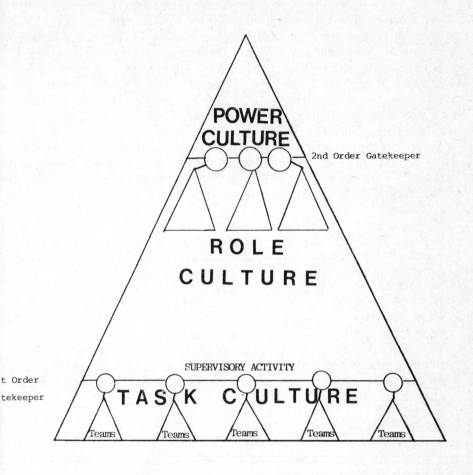

Figure 3.16　Three culture organisation

position of power. In fact, the evidence from the interviews suggests that a third cultural level exists in social service organisations, that of a power culture.

Persons involved in power activities concentrate at the top of the department. Their principal function is to maintain the status and position of the department in the power struggles that occur between themselves and directors of other departments in the local authority, between the senior managers within the SSD and the elected representatives. It is understandable that facilitating interpersonal relationships, manipulating others and handling grievances are a more comfortable experience, as the manager is likely to be the controlling or mediating influence in the situation. However, liaising with other departments and organisations; joint planning functions and administering policies involves far less control on the part of the manager and greater involvement in bargaining situations. Negotiating as opposed to facilitating, is far more of a demanding and stressful experience for individuals.

Figure 3.16 shows the two levels of gatekeepers. The first order level is represented by the supervisory grades as they operate at the boundary between the task culture and role culture. The *second order gatekeepers* are likely to be represented by the Assistant Directors because of their responsibility to liaise between the various units within the SSD and between the department and other organisations. Their work in terms of liaison, planning and delegation is to maintain an acceptable balance between the SSDs and other interested bodies. In this way, the department can function relatively effectively without undue pressure being placed on persons lower in the organisation. The second order gatekeepers operate at the boundary between the role culture and the power culture.

Career development

Two social psychologists Pritchard and Karasick (1973) state that congruence between individual needs and organisational values is important in predicting behaviour. What they mean is that in trying to understand the behaviour and attitudes of people in organisations, it is necessary to identify how the individual and the organisation are reconciled. Mumford (1970) states that the problem centres around the fit between the individual and the organisation. The results of our studies indicate that 'fit' is geared towards organisational requirements rather than professional social work development. The climate surrounding people's jobs is seen as supportive in terms of career development within the existing hierarchy. This involves administrative activity which people find undesirable in the short-term but know that promotional opportunities exist in the long-term. A hierarchical

110

career is the only fit possible in a situation where the role culture dominates the hierarchy.

For the individual wishing to embark on a career in the social services, it will be necessary to adjust to differences in both work practise and in attitudes towards work, from the task culture to the role culture. It would be exceedingly difficult for an individual to be effective in a managerial role, including that of supervisor, if he or she could not identify with the norms of the hierarchical organisation. Managerial work necessitates attending meetings, monitoring and co-ordinating the work of others, re-defining authority relationships, developing procedures and standards of work, establishing rules for the settlement of disputes etc. Over time, the roles in the hierarchy and not the individuals occupying the roles, will become the centre of discussion. Generalisations are likely to be made about social workers in terms of their behaviour and exhibited attitudes towards work, rather than discussion about particular individuals and their strengths and merits. In fact, less emphasis is likely to be placed on individuals whether they be clients, colleagues, superiors or subordinates and far greater emphasis on policies, resource allocation, longer term plans and data collection. The ultimate objective will be to maintain the organisation in a stable state.

What is learnt?

All human beings who have to work within an organisation are learning about their surrounding environment. Quite naturally, they learn how to do well in their job, how to inter-relate with colleagues and subordinates, how to pass information to interested parties and also how to withhold information. In essence, people are learning to react to each other and the situation within which they operate. People pick up cues and offer responses in return, and the degree to which a response is appropriate depends on the norms and values determining that situation.

For example, a supervisor whose work pattern we observed, stated that a particular responsibility of his was to ensure that certain forms were completed by the social workers in his team, given to him which he in turn had to pass on to his superior. This simple process was fraught with ambiguity. The social workers because of the constraints they faced, were late in passing to the senior social worker the information he required. The senior social worker was working within a time constraint in that the information was required of him every Friday. He feared retribution for an activity which he did not recognise as his responsibility. It would have been unlikely that the situation would have improved had he adopted an autocratic/authoritarian style with the social workers. Hence, he feared the consensus style of management and yet also feared to avoid it. Any individual that has to tolerate such contradiction for any length of time will fail to understand the problem and come to believe that he cannot discuss his problem situation with anyone else. It is no surprise that a number of senior social workers felt they were being undermined. It is equally no surprise that managers in SSDs were unable to understand why the seniors should feel threatened.

The senior social worker in the example above, by the fact that he occupied the position he did, naturally had to accept both the positive and negative aspects of his work. In accepting his job as it stood, the senior social worker established a *psychological contract* which made it possible for colleagues, superiors and subordinates to relate to him with ease although he may not have felt comfortable. Every psychological contract contains certain psychological messages and until the true nature of the messages are understood, problems at work will never be fully confronted.

From the studies reported in this chapter, certain messages can be identified that are contradictory. These psychological messages are presented in Table 3.8. For example, examine message 1. To take initiative with a client and act as each social worker thinks best in difficult situations, would seem a natural requirement of social worker/ client interaction. However, the message offered to a social worker on leaving the organisation to meet his client, is to remain within the rules and regulations already established (role culture). To take too much initiative with clients may involve crossing into someone else's area of responsibility and upsetting other agreements already made. The third message from the power culture, is make sure that the current situation is not upset. It has taken so long to manage the situation to its present position that senior management would feel threatened if the status quo were disturbed.

Because such fundamental inconsistencies exist, it is virtually impossible to surface basic problems for discussion. The inability to discuss inconsistencies is due to the presence of conflicting norms and the fact that individuals identify with different norms. People who identify with different norms talk in a different psychological language and require time to develop competence at being able to speak meaningfully to each other. However, the organisational position of persons in the hierarchy and the intergroup norms do not encourage them to develop such competence.

For example, it is likely that persons occupying managerial positions will be able to identify with those in social work positions when conflict arises. The objectives of each group in the conflict situation and the terminology used to justify the stand taken by each party, are likely to have little or no common ground. Those working in a task

Table 3.8

The messages

	Task culture		Role culture		Power culture
1.	Take initiative with clients	1.	Don't break the rules	1.	Don't threaten my position
2.	Be participative	2.	Work within your role constraints	2.	Support me in my actions
3.	Forward planning for future requirements	3.	Recognition, rewards and punishment are only offered for present performance	3.	I set the scene you do it
4.	Say if you make a mistake	4.	Sanctions must be applied for all errors	4.	Make sure it's only a small mistake
5.	Consider your colleagues in your team	5.	Think of the organisation as a whole	5.	You're lucky you got a job with us
6.	I take pride in my work	6.	Do what is required of you	6.	What I have to do for you lot

culture will probably champion the rights of individuals and small groups (including themselves), professional identity and the freedom to develop social work activities without bureaucratic interference. The response from management will be to question whether social worker demands fit with the longer term plans already in operation. Even if it is generally agreed that management should change its plan, the insurmountable difficulties in altering plans or doing anything new because of constraints imposed upon the department, will prevent any real progress in the negotiations between the two sides. The constraints may take the form of budgetary control or the inflexibility of organisation structure plans.

As can be seen, the language used by the two groups is aimed at quite different ends and these ends represent different group norms and personal values. It matters little whether qualified social workers enter into management or not; as the demands of the situation require changes in the work attitude and work practice of those who leave the task culture and enter the role culture.

Argyris and Schon (1978) state that in order for people to function in situations that encapsulate built-in contradictions, skills in gamesmanship develop amongst the actors involved. The playing of games is as much a need to protect oneself, as it is a strategy to maximise gains for oneself. Inevitably, the games centre on stimulating deception in order to maintain secrets amongst the select few, avoid any retribution for errors made and hide errors that are incorrectable.

As Argyris and Schon (1978) indicate, the one consequence of gamesmanship is the development of mistrust. Where mistrust abounds, senior management would respond by increasing the number of procedures for control, and be more directive in installing a system of rewards and penalties for all persons in the organisation. In the 'Study of organisational structure in nine SSDs', (p 67), the results indicate greater hierarchical control and increasing formality of procedure, with the senior social workers providing the gatekeeper service between two cultures. Their job is to introduce and maintain control over persons in the task culture.

For those within the task culture, the results of such action from superiors will induce a defensive response. People are far more likely to check their work so as not to be 'caught out' as opposed to checking work in order to maintain high professional standards. Work begins to develop negative connotations in that any system of checks and balances is not to maintain control of quality, but as a defence against others.

The more controls are applied, the more defensive becomes the response of the individual, reaching a stage of management by crisis. Management may talk in terms of 'how to keep the lads on their toes' to which subordinates respond by ensuring that their particular unit or department is administratively watertight. In Appendix 3, the assistant director states:

> I have learnt that we are local government officers first and
> a social worker second. So therefore, there are constraints
> to begin with that nobody can act outside the law and
> nobody can act outside their policy.

Factors such as mistrust, defensiveness, management by crisis, ineffective decision making and an inability to change, feed on each other and re-inforce each other to devalue the competence of the individual. In such situations, there is a great danger that people who displayed high levels of competence at their professional tasks will be unable to maintain a high skill level. Situations of mistrust and defensiveness reduce the level of initiative and intuition required for problem solving. Meeting new challenges can become more problematic each time a new situation arises. Poor feedback on task performance leads to a decrease in confidence which in turn will make future problem solving less effective, leading to a counter productive stage of an increase in the skills of gamesmanship.

Being 'over-concerned' about not doing anything wrong inhibits initiative. Over-concern with one's department or unit will lead to interdepartmental rivalry. Interdepartmental rivalries are likely to fester and increase, whilst flexibility for change and co-operation between departments is likely to decrease.

Summary

By analysing culture at the organisation, group and individual level, three cultures are identified — task, role and power cultures. Individuals working within one culture hold different personal beliefs about such issues as work, employment and professionalism, to persons operating within the other cultures. It is recognised that relationships between persons in the three different cultures are unlikely to be harmonious. Consequently 'gatekeepers' are identified at the team leader and assistant director levels, whose function is to act as a bridge, or link, between persons who operate within the separate cultures.

Career development within SSDs is oriented towards satisfying organisational (role culture) requirements as opposed to the demands of professional social work (task culture) development. People who wish to develop a career within SSDs feel that they can only be promoted up the hierarchy. No other substantial reward is seen as being offered for developing skills in 'professional' social work.

A question is asked, namely, 'What are people learning about their work and organisation?' It is considered that personnel within SSDs are learning to cope with ambiguity and contradictions. The contradictions arise from having people working in the same organisation, but under three different cultural umbrellas. The demands made upon individuals who work within one cultural setting may be in direct conflict with the personal beliefs and values of those who work in a different cultural grouping. A table is drawn up, identifying the psychological messages emanating from the three cultures. Any individual in SSDs has to take into account these messages when involved in any professional or departmental activities.

Because such inconsistencies exist within SSDs, free communication between colleagues, superiors and subordinates is considered difficult, if not impossible. Further, because people at different levels within the organisation hold different beliefs about work and the objectives they should fulfill, it is likely that skills in gamesmanship between superiors and subordinates will develop.

From research work in other organisations, one identified consequence of gamesmanship is the development of mistrust between people. Where little trust exists between persons of different managerial levels, senior management is likely to respond by increasing the number of rules and regulations in order to ensure their control over the situation. Under such circumstances, people at the lower end of the organisation are likely to respond by trying to evade control or to ensure that they 'cannot be caught out' by making their work administratively watertight. In these circumstances, work is not seen in a positive light for the system of formal checks and balances is not there to maintain control of quality of work, but as a defence against others. In situations where mistrust and defensiveness between people have become a norm, then the level of initiative and intuition required for solving quite complex problems is reduced in each individual. Further, meeting any new challenges will become problematic for senior management may respond by increasing the number of controls because of their distrust of social workers.

PART II

PRESSURES TOWARDS WHAT ACTION?

The results of the studies described in part I (chapter 3) of this book indicate that the respondents perceive their departments as having a centralised authority system backed by substantial formality of procedure. Further, formal relationships are seen as complex but oriented towards organisational complexity as opposed to professional, vocational complexity.

Senior social workers are identified as providing a quality control service over the activities of social workers but with greater emphasis on administrative procedures than on professional client/social worker relationships. In addition, three distinctly different organisational cultures are identified as operating simultaneously in each department, namely task, role and power cultures. An individual working in any part of the organisation will be influenced by the culture that dominates his/her organisation domain. Most people accept the culture that surrounds them and by accepting that culture, they internalise certain values and norms. These values and norms will then determine how they view and react to work, their place of employment and peers and superiors. The conclusion reached in chapter 3 is that the presence of three distinctly different cultures within one organisation is problematic.

The results also indicate how similar SSDs are to other organisations. The key factor is size of organisation. With their rapid growth, social services are now exhibiting similar problems to other organisations such as engineering companies, commercial banks, health service organisations, and even academic institutions. All of the above examples are companies and organisations of which I have personal experience, either as a consultant or researcher. Similar to social services, personnel in the above companies have expressed frustration over the centralised and formalised systems in operation and the perceived inability of groups within the organisation to be able to accept the work attitude and practise of others.

What of solutions to these problems? (See the macro-micro organisation development model on p. 121). In order to confront the problems that SSDs are currently facing and will have to face in the future, a two pronged approach is required. First, it is necessary to question whether the current design of social service organisations is appropriate. Does management have to tamper with and alter the current structures, procedures and information systems to meet newly recognised needs? The answer given in chapter 4, is an emphatic yes. The design strategies suggested in chapter 4 are aimed at the macro-level, i.e. the total organisation. The issue of whether to centralise or de-centralise is addressed with a note on what changes will realistically take place if either policies are adopted. The need for an accurate management information system is identified. The basic principles of management information systems are listed and hints are offered as to what is required in installing such a system. The need to re-organise casework practise in teams is discussed. The recommendation made is that professional multi-disciplinary teams sponsored by both SSDs and health authorities should be seriously considered. The need for competent internal and external consultants is deemed important. Case examples are offered of two SSDs who did not make proper use of their internal consultants. Finally, in chapter 4, the question whether another re-organisation is necessary, is addressed.

Chapter 5 concentrates at the micro-level, starting with an examination of the problems managers in SSDs have to currently face. SSDs are large, diverse organisations and it is vital that team leaders and higher level managers develop trust in each others capabilities. Without that trust, competent task performance is unlikely to occur. Further, it is probable that quite a number of people in SSDs will experience stress as part of their work. Persons most likely to be affected by stress are identified and certain warning symptoms of stress are listed. Most managers in SSDs face the problem of having to reconcile conflicting and contrasting demands made on them. It is necessary that they cope with that ambiguity. Part of the coping process involves developing skills in acting 'politically' within the organisation. Four sets of political tactics are identified. Part of being managerially politically astute, involves each manager in being able to identify his natural style. Four separate styles are discussed. Finally, the need for planned management development training is emphasised.

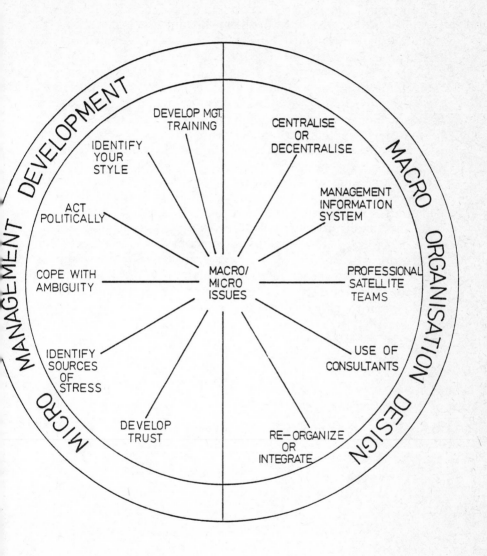

Part II — Macro-micro organisation development model

4 Design of social service organisations

The period of innovative organisational design for the social services was during the periods of re-organisation, 1970 to 1973. A new type of social service organisation had come into being to try and meet the needs of communities. For all those involved, it was a creative period of time.

However, it is not necessary to experience national re-organisation in order to become involved in organisation design activities. Most managers find themselves in the process of continually re-designing their section, department, division or even total organisation. Over the last decade, most, if not all directors of SSDs must have found themselves justifying their establishment to a higher authority. In order to develop a complete picture of the organisation, personnel in middle and senior management positions have to spend substantial periods of time drafting and re-drafting organisational charts, re-defining individual areas of authority and responsibility, designing office layout and putting forward budgets in order to acquire additional personnel and equipment. With this information, the director of the department would be armed to argue for the continued development of his establishment.

Consequently, most personnel in SSDs are involved in the process of designing or re-designing their organisation. Some are involved in macro-issues, such as the mission and purpose of SSDs, whilst others are more concerned with micro issues such as budgeting for office furniture and decor. The process of continually re-designing the organisation is natural. It is impossible for any organisation to stand still as changes are constantly occurring outside, both in the market place and the com-

123

munity. However in order to design or re-design the organisation, reliable and relevant data is necessary from which policy design decisions can be made. The problem most organisations face, is recognising and gathering that type of data.

The research studies described in chapter 3, form the data base for the design recommendations that are made in this chapter. Five areas of organisational design are identified:

1 Centralisation or decentralisation.
2 Developing an effective management information system (MIS).
3 Developing professional multi-disciplinary teams.
4 Using consultants (importance of third parties).
5 Integrating current activities and practise, or planning for further re-organisation.

Centralisation/decentralisation

Every SSD works according to some form of design. Formal organisation structure plans exist, identifying a hierarchy of roles, with job titles, job descriptions and descriptions of the authority inherent in each role. The final design will not be found on one sheet of paper but is likely to be a mixture of different plans that come together to form a complex matrix structure.

Once the design is fixed, cannot it be left alone so that people can get on with their job? Probably not, for in trying to get the design right, senior management is juggling with two conflicting policies simultaneously — the need to standardise and the need to diversify. The reasons for standardisation are threefold: reduction of costs; ease of communication by working to a common set of procedures; and control over work, so that both the way work is done (the process) and the results of that work (quality of products or service) can be monitored.

Equally, senior management has to allow for sufficient flexibility in the system for it to be able to adequately respond to changes in the community.

The degree of flexibility within the system depends on the goals of the department. Certain goals can be consciously established. For example, the system can be arranged to be sufficiently flexible so that social workers at the lower end of the organisation can feed information to senior management, so that managers can re-evaluate their original goals. However, other goals are an expression of identity and cannot be introduced or taken away according to changes in policy. The goals of individual teams or groups, especially if backed by a strong professional method, can be different to the intended goals of the department. The goals of the profession and the goals of the department are often not congruent.

There is a danger that the greater the range of diverse goals that exist within the organisation, the more senior management would wish to gain greater control over both resources and people. This may in turn, undermine the role of managers at area offices as control remains at head office. Middle managers occupying a geographic peripheral position to head office, may then strive for a redistribution of control over resources.

The arguments for greater conformity of procedures or greater diversity of goals and action have been couched in the centralisation/decentralisation arguments. A large number of SSDs have recently attempted to re-organise, by centralising or decentralising their control system. As centralisation/decentralisation are important policy issues, it is worth examining them. Child (1977) neatly summarises the points in favour of both options.

For centralisation

1 Simplicity of co-ordination will occur if decisions are made at one point or amongst a small group.
2 Senior management will have a broader perspective on developments within the organisation and maintain conformity of already established policies. In terms of keeping up to date with recent developments, they are better able to adjust to any changes in order to provide for the interests of the organisation. This will avoid loss of control to people at lower levels who would be making decisions which are optimal for their group or sub-unit but sub-optimal for the organisation as a whole.
3 Centralisation of control and procedures provides a way of helping the various functional areas in the organisation — research and development, fieldwork activities, administration of residential establishments — to maintain an appropriate balance. This occurs by centralising decisions on resource allocation, functional policies, targets etc.
4 Centralisation can economise on managerial overheads by avoiding duplication of activities or resources if similar activities are being carried out independently in divisions or sub-units.
5 Through preventing the segmentation of management to the lower levels of the organisation, there is greater justification for the employment of specialists who can act as consultants to the various functions and levels within the organisation.

This service would be difficult to account for expenditure-wise in a decentralised system as there could be substantial duplication of consultant resources.

6 It is commonly held that top managers have proven themselves by the time that they reach a senior position. Although a point in favour of centralisation, there is a danger that management can adopt the attitude that because we are at the top, we are right.

7 Crisis situations often require strong leadership to cope with external and internal pressures. Centralisation of power and control of procedures focuses on a key person or group. Thus arises the opportunity for speedy decision making and control over communication and co-ordination.

For decentralisation

1 Delegation can reduce the amount of stress and overload experienced by senior management, especially when operating in large scale, complex organisations. It is well understood that when senior management becomes over-loaded, then the effective control they exercise becomes diminished. Rather than just becoming involved in poorly thought through plans and speedy decision making, delegation can relieve some of their burden, leaving senior management to spend more time on policy issues and long-term planning. Delegation is not simply a clear cut decision by senior management to increase the number of decision-making tasks of managers at lower levels. It is more a process of sharing responsibility by inviting other members of the management hierarchy to participate in decisions that they used to make.

2 It has long been held by behavioural scientists that the motivation of employees will increase the higher the degree of discretion and control they can apply over their work. The opportunity to make decisions and be involved can help to provide personal satisfaction and commitment for the individual. An assumption is made that with greater personal freedom, individual goals will broadly be in line with those of the corporate entity. In situations of delegated power, the matching of personal goals and corporate goals is more likely but delegation can be severely tested in situations where people's work is independent of each other. The problem there, is to sufficiently motivate people to co-ordinate their activities without too much central direction.

3 Organisations that are too large or growing, need managers

who are able to cope with uncertainty because of the immense number of complex tasks that have to be performed. It is impossible for one person or small groups of people to supervise such complex activities simultaneously. Delegation therefore can assist the development of management by widening the on-the-job skills of managers and hence create a healthy stock of persons capable of senior management positions.

4 Delegation generally allows for greater flexibility by providing for less rigid responses to change at the operative levels in the organisation. Decisions do not have to be referred up the hierarchy.

5 For social services, the above is particularly pertinent. An individual, actively involved with a community problem and aware of local conditions, should be capable of making better decisions than a senior manager, several levels removed, where information about events is transmitted through the written word. As long as the person involved in local problems is aware of and accepts corporate policies, delegation makes sense.

6 By establishing relatively independent sub-units within an organisation where middle management and supervisors are held responsible for operations, delegation can result in more effective controls and performance measurements. Separate spheres of responsibility can be identified and control systems applied to these units in order to provide adequate feedback to higher management. Costs can be identified and allocated to particular operations, rendering specific responsibility on specific persons or units. Greater self-responsibility and self-direction are required of people in such circumstances.

A simple decision to centralise or decentralise is impossible, for the choice between the two can only be made in the light of specific conditions and circumstances. These conditions will vary from:

a) the overall purpose of the organisation;
b) the capacity of senior management to conceive of a new type of organisation;
c) the skills and attitudes of subordinates;
d) the overall size, divisional size (if applicable) and geographic dispersion of the organisation;
e) the efficiency and accuracy of the organisation's planning, control and information systems;
f) the time restrictions that accompany decisions made in the field or within the organisation. For example, in order for

an action to be effective in the field, is it appropriate for a decision to be made on the spot based on professional judgement, or is the situation sufficiently flexible in terms of time, to allow for a decision to be referred upwards to senior management?

g) the degree to which subordinates can accept and are in turn motivated by making their own decisions;

h) the conditions external to the organisation that will strongly influence its operation, such as government requirements, trade union objectives and local community conditions.

Some SSDs have attempted to overcome problems of poor motivation by decentralising. However, a common and mistaken assumption is that by decentralising, persons working at the lower end of the organisation will gain greater satisfaction because they feel more involved. This need not necessarily be so, for decentralisation is only the formal way of coping with numerous complex tasks. Something additional to decentralisation needs to be done, because the problems emanating from the centralised system will continue to show themselves as before. By changing the attitudes and work behaviour of the persons who have to operate within the decentralised system, then decentralisation has a chance of success. People must feel that they have to relate to others in a different way in the decentralised system, than they did in the centralised system. Such a change of attitude and behaviour can be brought about by some form of human relations training which adds to the existing policy of decentralisation. The training may consist of seminars, workshops, unstructured group work, project group studies and individual counselling. Different types of human relations training are discussed in chapter 5.

Management information system (MIS)

How to develop a good MIS is an important consideration for any large, complex organisation. The aim of the organisation is to work to an overall plan by ensuring that the activities of the units and divisions within the organisation merge together. The process of merging can only be satisfactorily achieved by installing an adequate communication and maintenance system.

A competent MIS should be the linking mechanism in organisations where diversity predominates. Diversity could relate to the different functions and activities that are performed, as well as to differences of values, attitudes and norms held by individuals and groups within the organisation.

We have seen from the studies in chapter 3 that three separate cultures are identified within SSDs. The results suggest that the predominant culture is the role culture. Persons who are role culture oriented, are strategically placed within the middle levels of SSDs, controlling most forms of communication up and down the department. Unless the information system primarily caters for the needs of persons within the role culture, they will not be able to provide an adequate service for people in the power and task cultures.

The objective to achieve by introducing an MIS, would be to fit together distinctly different cultures through a common and acceptable information system. For SSDs, the fundamentally different cultures are those at the bottom and middle of the organisation; the task and role cultures. The task culture is geared towards greater diversity whereas the role culture aims to achieve greater uniformity. Any system that enhances communication and also maintains control of activities in the hands of management is worth considering. It offers persons in the task culture freedom to develop their own line of enquiry over their activities and yet be balanced by uniformity of procedure.

What practical objectives have to be achieved if an MIS is to satisfy the demands of task and role cultures within SSDs?

To improve the effectiveness of long-term planning. In an industrial organisation, the data for long-term planning is easier to identify; for example, sales data can be broken down by sales within one geographic area, or time taken for a range of products to be sold. In social work, the situation is different. The data required for future planning is difficult to define and always open to question. This makes presentation of data to senior management a problem. In the literature, the only writer who discusses data analysis, in terms of utilisation for an information system is Matilda Goldberg.

Goldberg and her team have published two articles which unfortunately have not had the impact they deserve. Her first article with David Fruin (Goldberg and Fruin 1976) gives the background to the Case Review System. Social work tasks are identified as being vast, vague and undifferentiated. In order to create stability in such diverse complexity, Goldberg and Fruin suggest that an urgent research need is the development of a systematic recording and reviewing system which provides basic information about social worker activities and their effect on different client groups. The 1976 article identifies the advantages of the case review system as:

a) enabling social workers to plan their work with individual clients;
b) assisting the process of supervision;
c) a management tool in the planning of field work services;
d) an information service offering up-to-date accounts con-

cerning the size, nature and scope of social work activities with different client groups.

Since then, Goldberg and her team (Goldberg *et al* 1978) have conducted practical research studies exploring some of their ideas. In a study of over 1,400 cases, Goldberg indicated that there exists a need to think again about what services to provide for long-term clients. The study showed that surveillance and review visiting was considered vital for a substantial number of cases.

Another finding was the uneven distribution of social work resources among different problem groups. For example, even though physically disabled groups outnumbered the child and family problems by two to one; the physically disabled made up 20 per cent of the allocated cases, whilst children and family problems accounted for 35 per cent of all individual case loads.

Further problems were identified in the way casework was practised with the frail and elderly, and chronically disturbed families. Overall, the examination of social work practise has led Goldberg to question the wisdom of the overall deployment of resources in SSDs. She recommends an information system that will provide accurate data for senior management to use for policy formulation, but provided for by field-workers.

Goldberg's recommendation provides a means of linking the task and role cultures. Data that was *tacit* (i.e. commonly understood by those involved but is difficult to express clearly) and is made *explicit* (laid down on paper and identified by pre-established criteria and categories) would satisfy the norms of both cultures. Such explicit data could then form the basis for developing financial resource estimates, upon which planning for the future is based. With emphasis being placed on explicit information does tacit information become unimportant? Not at all, for tacit information is the basis upon which explicit information is built and hence, social workers become the data source of senior management decisions. (For further explanation of tacit and explicit information, see 'Professional satellite teams', p 132.)

To improve the effectiveness of managerial control. In certain situations, speed of provision of information may be more important than accuracy of information. Probably, a major problem for any organisation that has a role and task culture operating side by side, is that information quickly needed by management is not rapidly forthcoming from those operating within the task culture. The application of a Goldberg type system could help in reducing the problem. If social workers adhere to a routine form filling process which they consider meaningful as opposed to an interference from management, then greater control over daily activities will occur.

To reduce conflict. An information system that links disinterested parties to each other, is likely to reduce the potential level of aggravation between the groups. First, all interested parties will know what is required of them and why. Second, individual persons can plan their workload for they know what type of information they have to gather and refer upwards. A nagging frustration at work is that people of all levels in the hierarchy may be asked to provide or find, information without any prior warning. Sometimes they do not know where to begin to search, and often do not know why the information is needed. Working to a common information system will help to reduce the level of conflict.

To improve the motivation of individuals. People who know what is expected of them, can plan for future events and know that what they are doing does have meaning and is purposeful. They are motivated to work within identified constraints where they are more certain of their position. One result in Chapter three showed that formality of procedure was not viewed as demotivating as supervisory control. The more people know as to what is required of them, the less the need for direct supervisory intervention. The knowledge that another person is checking your work for errors rather than working with you, does lead to defensive and subversive behaviour. In such circumstances, the prime work objective of an individual is to make sure he is not 'found out' even though there may be nothing to 'find out'.

Professional satellite teams

In this section, a recommendation is made that SSDs, possibly together with health authorities, should be considering the development of multi-disciplinary teams which I term *professional satellite teams*. Before identifying the basic principles of professional satellite teams, a case is made showing what problems exist within SSDs and the community and how they would be overcome by the creation of these teams.

In the last section p. 130, reference was made to tacit and explicit information. It was stated that any management information system has to be based on explicit information. If the MIS is to work throughout the organisation, then whatever explicit information is asked for, has to be seen as an acceptable request by all members of the organisation. As the likely dominant culture in SSDs is the role culture, then the explicit information generated is used to increase the effectiveness of the role culture.

Does that then mean that tacit information is used only to develop accurate explicit information? In order to answer the question, a further explanation of tacit information is required. Tacit information, as previously stated, is that information which is commonly understood but at the same time is difficult to express clearly. As shown in Table 4.1 tacit information is unclear, depends to a degree on generalisation, is verbally communicated, and problem centred. In contrast, explicit information is clear, distinct, oriented towards functional structures and organisation systems, and is easily communicated on paper.

For example, anyone operating in poorly defined situations utilises tacit information. Social workers working with families will for a time, be confused as to what action to take. Their feelings and perceptions about the situation will be unclear, as the information they are identifying is ambiguous and confusing. Through discussion with other social workers and each individual workers 'gut feel', a picture will slowly emerge indicating what action to take next.

Consequently, it is not easy to change information from being tacit to explicit, as tacit information is by its very nature, confusing and ambiguous. Further, the communication of tacit information is not by the written word, but by word and mouth from one social worker to another, relying heavily on the use of analogies in order to explain situations.

Table 4.1

Information
Explicit and tacit information

Tacit	Explicit
Unclear	Clear
Comparative	Distinct
Generalised	Reductive
Problem centred	Function oriented
Verbally communicated	Graphically communicated
Small group oriented	System oriented
Experiential	Controlled

By generating an effective information flow system which produces explicit information, there is always a danger that tacit information becomes of secondary importance. Yet, tacit information is vital for the continued practise of social work. Goldberg *et al* (1978) indicated that there exist twice as many physically disabled and elderly cases as children and family cases, but in fact, twice as much time was spent with children and families. Namely, in actual fieldwork practise, twice the amount of time is spent utilising tacit information as opposed to explicit information.

Tacit information is dependent on the sensitivities and feelings of each individual person to different situations. Organisations that are restrictive and controlling in nature will tend to lower the morale of their employees. Hence, people's ability to use tacit information will be reduced, because they will be asked to explicitly justify their activity and not explore and develop into new areas. Consequently, understanding the attitude social workers hold towards their employing organisation and clients, is of paramount importance for it gives an indication of how well tacit information is utilised. We have seen in chapter 3 that SSDs are viewed by their personnel as being centralised and formalised in structure with increasing standardisation of work, tasks and careers. If social work treatment involves clarification of subjective experiences and meanings, are SSDs in the way they are currently structured, assisting or hindering the process of casework intervention?

Some writers have hypothesised that the relationship between the client and the helping agency is the real problem area. Humes and Kennedy (1970) suggest that social workers involved with schools should be given greater freedom in the planning of school curricula and hence, greater positive involvement in student development. Hartmann (1969) agrees, stating that caseworkers should have greater involvement in the dynamic here and now interaction that takes place between the individual and his particular social context. Hartmann is implying that caseworkers should have far greater personal identity with their client situation than with their employing organisation.

Arbuckle (1969) indicates that counsellors working in authoritarian organisations eventually adopt authoritarian attitudes.

Belok's (1970) study of teachers, indicates that perceived lack of freedom, concerning daily work decisions induces feelings of alienation directed towards the employing organisation and daily work. Gowler and Parry (1979) develop the theme further and state that many professionals face the 'cruciform effect' which highlights the dilemma between taking risks and being innovative with clients and being held accountable by the organisation.

With such evidence, a number of writers (Hersch 1966) have asked whether coping with the processes of disengagement (alienation) will require a re-examination of our models of treatment as well as a re-appraisal of administrative hierarchies? Taking up Hersch's point, are social workers alienated to the stage where their skills to practise casework are diminishing?

In a recent article by Morris in *Community Care* (1979), NSPCC inspectors were identified as having a Victorian image. The reason for this image was due to the bureaucratic and restrictive nature of the NSPCC organisation such as not having a system of standby payments or time off in lieu; a total restriction on inspectors working for any other organisation in their own time; apparent restrictions on political activities; lack of secondment facilities for professional social work training courses; and so the list of grievances continued. The point Morris was making, was that the restrictive and controlling nature of the NSPCC organisation was lowering morale (i.e. reducing the ability to use tacit information) whereby, each individual ended up just inspecting and not acting as an experienced caseworker. In fact, the new director recognised the influence the organisation was having on its inspectorate and stated:

> The time's come . . . for the Society to make the break and allow its social workers — why do they still call them inspectors? — to practise more permissive social work without the controls which are very much Victorian.

Let us examine another problem area; that of battered children. Marran and Buchanan (1979) identified the changes in the pattern of non-accidental injuries to children in Leeds between 1969 and 1978.

Table 4.2

Non-accidental injuries in Leeds
(1969—1978)

Type of injury	No. of children	
	1969—73	1974—78
Superficial injuries	117	194
Bone	37	25
Brain and eyes	37	3
Death	5	1
Total*	117	196

* Note: many children have several kinds of injury so that the total adds up to more than the number of injured children.

Table 4.2 shows an increase in the number of cases of battered children but a decrease in the number of serious cases. Both trends can be explained by the fact that both social workers and doctors are now more aware of non-accidental injury to children and hence, are able to intervene more rapidly and effectively. Previously undetected symptoms of non-accidental injury no longer remain undetected, but as a direct consequence, the recorded number of injuries to children has increased. Equally, the number of fatal injuries have decreased.

With this evidence, Marran and Buchanan plead for greater co-operation between social workers and doctors, because without that partnership, certain injuries, although detected by doctors, will go unregistered as non-accidental injuries. For example, hospital doctors are often asked to examine young children with skull fractures. Skull fractures are surprisingly common forms of injury. There may be little or no sign of injury on the outside of the skull but further examination will show a fracture. Even more surprising is that it is sometimes impossible to establish how the fracture occurred. With such uncertainty surrounding such serious injury, a social report from a social worker is vital. Unless doctors know of social workers to whom they can quickly refer clients for close supervision, then a family at risk can slip through the net.

Let us turn to more serious cases of non-accidental fatal injury to children. In Table 4.3, five children are identified that suffered non-accidental fatal injury. The inquiry reports and other documentation on each child provide interesting reading. First, in all five cases, comments such as inadequate support services, or insufficient training or insufficient knowledge to help children at risk or the inability of the field worker and department to provide an adequate service, were made by interested outside parties. In all cases, the SSD involved seemed to be made to look incompetent. In fact, in the Wayne Brewer case, Somerset social services department (the authority involved) held an effective 'At Risk Register', which since the inquiry, has been reported as administratively more effective. But how does having an 'At Risk Register' assist the *process* of treatment? An 'At Risk Register' informs the caseworker who is at risk, but does not tell him what to do in the at-risk situation.

Second, in the minority of cases, the employing department came out as supportive of the field workers involved, after holding their own internal inquiry. In the majority of cases, senior management (including elected local counsellors on the social services committee) demanded retribution for what were considered to be errors of judgement on the part of the fieldworkers.

Third, in all cases, the fieldworkers involved stated that they felt themselves to be isolated, or unable to cope, or poorly trained and sometimes found themselves in the position of having to make decisions whilst not being fully aware or fully in control of the situation. Perhaps, worse still, they found it difficult to communicate their feelings of isolation to others. In the Carly Taylor case, the report stated that the senior social worker should have made certain decisions about the child long before fatality occurred. Specifically, the senior social worker should have organised a meeting bringing together the relevant helping agencies to discuss the Taylor family. Whether the senior social worker was at fault or not, it becomes apparent reading the report, that the person felt himself to be isolated and somehow

135

Table 4.3

Autopsy of tragedies

Child	Comments about the SSD from interested outside parties	Reaction of Senior Management in SSD	Comments from social workers involved
Susan Auckland	Identify person responsible — acting area team leader. Social workers made to look incompetent.	Suspicion then, now denied, that persons responsible in the department would be suspended.	Feeling that people outside do not really understand. Required a stronger support service.
Wayne Brewer	Identify why things went wrong. Certain actions social workers should have taken but did not.	Held internal enquiries with the aim of honestly establishing the facts. Strongly supported those workers involved.	Appreciated support from department. Now have an effective 'At Risk' register. Social worker felt he did not have sufficient knowledge to help children at risk.
Karen Spencer	Inquiry held. Social workers felt that they were made to look incompetent. Organisational changes recommended.	Management felt responsible. Field staff felt greater support from colleagues than from the hierarchy.	People do not understand problems field workers face in dealing with children at risk. Require greater support service.
Maria Colwell	Blamed SSD. Suspicion that social worker was singled out and scape-goated.	Little support for the social worker involved from the SSD. Suspicion of retribution directed at the social worker.	Social worker felt isolated in the decisions she made. Report indicated that internal organisational account-ability and responsibility were somewhat confusing.
Carly Taylor	Blamed complicated intake of client procedures in SSD. Suspicion that senior social worker was singled out and scape-goated.	Little support for senior social worker. Suspicion of retribution directed at senior social worker. Director of SSD stated senior social worker was in the wrong pay grade.	Senior social worker felt isolated in the decisions made. Report indicated that internal organisational accountability and responsibility were somewhat confusing.

unable to make a major decision on what to do next.

What the cases in Table 4.3 indicate, is that the ability to utilise tacit information is restricted. The only way to develop a clear picture from confusing subjective experiences and interpretations of situations, is to talk to persons of similar professional interests. Simply stating that more training is required is of little use, as social workers are asked to use their intuition to problem solve in acutely problematic situations. What is required is a co-counselling service for social workers, i.e. a service where professionals counsel each other to develop their problem solving skills.

'True' professional communication can only be achieved in professional teams that are oriented towards developing a task culture. In a role culture dominated organisation, the values and norms of task oriented professionals will not show through. In fact, what becomes noticeable are the problem symptoms identified in Table 4.3, i.e. feelings of isolation, inability to make decisions, confusion over task responsibilities and over lines of accountability and authority, scapegoating by senior management when things begin to go wrong.

It is important to recognise the value of tacit information as the dominant form of communication within task oriented cultures. In order for SSDs to stimulate greater use of tacit information in field work practice it means creating *professional satellite teams* working apart from the parent organisation. The principles under which such teams would operate are:

1 Encourage persons of different professional backgrounds to become team members, e.g. general practitioners, psychiatrists, psychologists, specialist or generic social workers, occupational therapists, health visitors, policemen etc.

2 Ensure that the team adopts a true task oriented culture by making decisions and acting independently of the parent organisation, e.g. SSDs or health authority.

3 The model of operation of the satellite teams has to be treatment oriented as opposed to working on more routine social work cases. Inspectorial activities, routine follow-up, adoption cases and court case duties, whether involving adults or children, should be left to the social workers employed within the SSD. All other cases, requiring long-term casework and medical skills should be referred to the professional team. This means that the specialist teams depend upon referrals from social workers, general practitioners and hospital based doctors. The aim of the team is to operate as a multi-disciplinary unit in an inter-disciplinary style and co-operate with relevant outside agencies.

4 There should be only one accountability line within the

team. The person at the head of the unit or team is account-able for the practises and activities of all personnel within the team.

5 Teams should be relatively small in size, with possibly one or more teams within the same geographic area.

6 Offices in which the teams are located should be set apart from the parent organisation.

7 Members of the team would work full-time within the team, possibly seconded from the parent organisation for periods of 1—3 years, or even be employed as permanent members of the team.

8 Generate a career hierarchy within the teams which indivi-dual professional members could strive to climb, based on competent work with clients. The hierarchy should be *shallow*, and whether at the top or bottom of the hierarchy, all members of the team are practitioners.

9 Professional teams have to be financially supported by local authorities and health authorities.

The evidence identified throughout this book, points to the need for developing multi-disciplinary teams that operate independently of the parent organisation. Such a setting will provide the climate for creative work with clients. Emphasis is placed on developing a professionally oriented task culture that will stimulate courageous as opposed to reckless, medical and casework treatment models. The lessons that can be learnt from the information in Tables 4.2 and 4.3 is that something additional to devising organisational rules and procedures as a response to emergencies, needs to be done to combat dramatic cases of social need.

The idea of developing an independent multi-disciplinary team is nothing new. Most GP practices operate a multi-disciplinary system with great success. The reason that GP practices are successful is that they operate a vocationally oriented, as opposed to an administratively oriented, hierarchy.

Police/Social Services Juvenile Bureau

In addition to GP's teams, one SSD has begun to experiment with multi-interdisciplinary professional teams. In 1979 in Exeter a unique five year experiment was initiated. An integrated operational unit consisting of police officers and social workers was established and called the 'Police/Social Services Juvenile Bureau'. J.B. Morgan, the Assistant Chief Constable of Devon and Cornwall, outlines in his paper (Morgan 1980), the four objectives of the bureau (p. 1):

1 To co-ordinate efforts to combat juvenile delinquency in

the city of Exeter.

2 To record and analyse criminal referrals and other actions relating to juveniles.
3 To develop more effective/preventive treatment policies.
4 To develop community and volunteer services in support of the statutory services.

It was recognised that both police and social services had a great deal to gain by fully co-operating over issues of juvenile delinquency. It was also recognised that a high degree of collaboration would involve developing a new type of organisation. In effect, it was recognised that in order to operate effectively in the community, a small, flexible organisation was required. In addition, differences in attitude and ideology between police and social workers could be confronted within such a setting. In an independent team setting, task culture oriented professionals seem to have overcome their basic differences.

However, some difficulties do not seem to have become overcome. The basic problems are not between police and social workers, but between the team and the parent organisations (task v role culture). In this case, the police seemed to have adjusted organisationally but not so with the social services. The problem has centred on the degree of authority in decision making delegated respectively to the senior policeman and the senior social worker in the bureau. From the outset, the police inspector in the bureau was given power of decision making on issues as, whether or not to contain a juvenile offender or to institute criminal court proceedings. On the social services side, the senior social worker, and the social workers are still responsible to the intake team of the SSD. Hence, there exists an imbalance of authority between the police and social services representatives on the team. A team director is required independent of both organisations.

A number of similar experiments are being conducted in Europe, in Hanover (Steinhilper 1980), for example. Yet, finding the organisational means to generate a truly task oriented culture, has largely not been recognised as an activity worth pursuing. In fact, Parsloe and Stephenson (1978) ask the question as to whether SSDs should pursue 'in-depth work or practical help?' There should, and can be, no either—or about the question. It is a matter of organising the organisation to allow both to flourish.

Importance of third parties

Parsloe and Stephenson (1978) pay special attention to a group of people known as advisors or consultants. An advisory or consultant type position is a common phenomena in most SSDs. However,

Parsloe's and Stephenson's research findings match my own; that in most authorities, the function and responsibilities of the consultants are unclear to the person occupying the role and also to other members of the hierarchy. Parsloe and Stephenson identified consultants in senior management positions — assistant directors and principle social workers — and those at the lower levels of the hierarchy having more narrowly defined tasks — intermediate treatment officers, pre-school play group officers, and fostering and adoptions officers.

The senior management advisors are specialists working with particular client groups such as children at risk, the handicapped, mentally ill, etc. The advisors assist all members of the hierarchy in offering advice, monitoring standards of work, developing services and providing consultation and support. Advisors at the lower end of the organisation are again experts in particular fields, e.g. officers specialising in the welfare of the blind. The social worker for the blind, provides a service to clients but further acts as a consultant to other social workers, informing them of the services available and of the administrative procedures involved in providing such a service.

It is no surprise that Parsloe and Stephenson record that others in the department express confusion as to the role and function of advisors and consultants. Let me attempt to clarify the situation. Consultants occupy a third party role and a third party is a person, or group of people, who assist the continued development of the organisation by helping to diagnose problem areas, generate new strategies, implement solutions and review the continuous process of change and development. Third party facilitators develop activities that are not the responsibility of any full time employee. A third party is the additional member to the superior/subordinate relationship.

Are third parties important? — yes they are vital! The research results in chapter 3 indicate that three distinctly different cultures are present within SSDs. Three groups of people work together and yet hold different personal beliefs and opinions about clients, the ethics of work, organisational hierarchies and professional and career loyalties. In such circumstances, the task of the third party is to provide cohesion to a diverse situation.

What is the role of the lower level advisors? Intermediate treatment officers, officers for the blind and adoption service officers not only provide specialist advice and guidance but have intimate knowledge of the administrative procedures necessary to set the required support service into action. This does not mean simply understanding which forms to complete, but knowing one's way around the administrative and legal complexities that must be taken into account before providing a specialist service. These officers provide an additional gatekeeper service between the task and role cultures. Although such a service is difficult to define, it is important in maintaining communication between persons in the task culture and role culture who would not otherwise easily understand the requirements of the other, when negotiating for the provision of a special service for particular clients.

Advisors in a senior management position such as assistant director (research and development) provide specialist advice and stimulate new ideas. The role of the assistant director (R & D) would be to gather data, identify new needs, argue for the provision of a new service and then assist in operationalising the new service. In fact, such senior consultants provide a valuable link between the power, role and task cultures. Gathering data to identify new needs has to be carried out within the task culture setting; arguing for the provision of new services must involve senior management (power culture) and identifying the rules and procedures for the operationalisation of the new service involves working with middle managers (role culture).

Would others in the hierarchy be able to provide a 'linking pin' service? Probably not. Even so, it is difficult to assess the positive contribution of third party agents. One way of identifying whether third parties play a valuable role or not, is to examine situations where little or poor use is made of consultants. Below are two case studies which examine situations where either consultant help was not available or was not competently utilised.

Metropolitan district social services department (N. England)

A director of a metropolitan district SSD attempted to decentralise the department; reduce the number of managerial posts in the organisation and increase the number of fieldwork posts. No redundancies or cut-backs were threatened. It was more a matter of changing the task responsibilities of certain lower and middle level managers from administration to social work activities. A number of consultant posts were created in order to provide the link between management and fieldworkers and to help develop new services.

The aim of the plan was to provide a professional fieldwork service with as little as possible emphasis on management. Whatever the merits of the new venture, the greater number of middle managers opposed the implementation of the plan. Their opposition was successful, and the director, frustrated by lack of progress, resigned. The successor could not see the merits of the former director's plan, nor could he understand the role of the consultants. The hierarchy was re-organised to more traditional lines and the consultant posts were changed to line management roles, to fit into the line hierarchy.

Not long after, during the period of intermittent strikes (1978/79), the social workers went on strike for the first time in the history of the department. A deeply held grievance was that they no longer had access to management and wished to establish a better line of communication. The strike ended having achieved little. Poor relations between management and the workforce remain to this day.

One assistant director had held a consultant role under the old scheme and had been involved in both policy making and implementation of strategies. The individual had been responsible for identifying new needs and suggesting means of operationalising services to meet these needs. As part of the policy to remove consultant type positions from the hierarchy, the individual assistant director was offered a line manager's job. As a result, most of the innovative research and development activities ceased.

Further, the assistant director in question was 'trusted' by the social workers. If any disputes arose, she was called (by both social workers and the former director) to act as a mediator. Since the individual accepted line responsibility social workers did not feel that the particular person had any mediating role to play in the current strike. Consequently, there was no one available to act as a go-between between the director and the social workers.

The consultants appointed in the original plan for decentralisation provided a valuable link between social workers and the managerial hierarchy. Once the consultants were removed, team leaders and senior social workers found they could not stimulate a poorly motivated workforce. It could be argued that had the original plan towards decentralisation not been put into practice, these sorts of problems would not have occurred. However, the original plan to decentralise was a response to increasingly poor social worker/management relationships.

The consultant role played by the assistant director is worth considering. The individual was given the freedom to examine current work practices within the department, search for new needs in the community, attempt to implement services to meet these needs and monitor their development. The pursuit of such activities involved the assistant director in meeting persons from all levels of the hierarchy. People felt that they could 'trust' the assistant director to understand their work problems and if necessary, negotiate on their behalf for facilities to improve the situation.

The removal of the consultant assistant director had two consequences. First, as stated, the generation of new ideas was reduced. Second, attempts by senior management to implement any new services were viewed with hostile suspicion. The personal link between individuals of different hierarchical levels had been lost.

When I last saw the director of the department, he described himself as the most isolated person in the department.

Rural county social services department (S. England)

A certain number of senior social workers in the county were trained in specialist social work skills. The training programmes proved to be so successful, that the senior social workers decided to hold meetings amongst themselves after their course. The meetings were, and are being held, in the senior social workers own time and at their own expense. At most of the senior social workers meetings, others such as consultant advisors were present, because the topics discussed were of general interest to all.

After some time, the divisional directors in the department began to feel increasingly threatened and expressed concern at the recurrance of these meetings. The consultant advisors were ordered by the divisional directors to report all developments that took place at the senior social workers meetings.

The senior social workers could not understand why their meetings were viewed with suspicion. Their objective was to review the standard of specialist services offered within the county and not to discuss or criticise the managerial hierarchy. Eventually, the director of the department became involved. At one meeting between the director, the divisional directors, and senior social workers, it was stated by the divisional directors that they considered the senior social workers to be discussing policy issues and not issues of specialist client care. The senior social workers denied that they discussed policy. They stated that their objective was to try and understand what needs in the community could be met by certain specialist services. Although meetings are continuing to the present day, both sides are resentful of each other and the original impetus of trying to understand and meet particular community needs has now been lost. In fact, I suspect that the senior social workers are continuing to meet more in defiance of the divisional directors than to discuss the improvement of specialist services.

This case is a classic example of a task/role culture conflict. Senior social workers were expected to remain within prescribed task responsibilities. To 'break set' generated problems in that the dominant group in the role culture, the divisional directors, felt that an essential part of their role had been taken over. Ideally, any changes in work practise in any part of the department should have been negotiated with the divisional directors. That did not take place. Consequently, senior social workers, whose concern was to improve service delivery to the community through negotiating changes in work practise, found substantial opposition to what they considered to be innovative ideas. Adaptation and change aimed at improving professional service is acceptable in task cultures, but quite unacceptable in role cultures.

The reason the consultant advisors seemed unable to facilitate better relationships between the two groups was that, although consultants in name, they were not consultants in practise. Research on my part showed that they behaved and were perceived by the senior social workers, as being inspectors. The consultant advisors were held directly accountable by the director who dictated where and when they should intervene. Consequently, few people trusted the consultant advisors and in reality no link existed between the task culture and role culture. As in most task/role culture conflicts, people communicated by direct confrontation, offering no room for maneouvre or compromise.

Outside consultants

Third parties need not just be internal consultants. External consultants can provide a valuable role in assisting and stimulating change in the organisation. Basically, there exist two types of external consultants; consultants who are available on an intermittent basis and assist in the process of problem searching; full time commercial consultants, who are hired to apply a standard solution to organisation problems.

Staff of university business schools are becoming increasingly popular as the intermittent type of consultant. They are capable of potentially long-term collaborative but intermittent relationships with organisations, as they are already employed by the business school. Hence, they provide a service to the client organisation only when necessary. Their function is to help identify new needs and jointly, with the organisation, develop strategies for change. A generally typical sequence of events would be:

a) a need is identified;
b) research is undertaken to provide data in order to diagnose the problem;
c) this data is offered to interested parties;
d) meaningful discussion may or may not take place, depending on the nature of the problem and the degree to which those involved wish to ignore or further develop thinking about the particular problem. If it is decided that discussion should take place, then the setting for the discussion has to be considered;
e) discussion could be developed at workshops, working parties formal courses with freedom for the participants to write a project, become involved in management meetings etc.;
f) a decision may be reached for action;
g) the parties involved are informed and grouped to develop strategy plans for change;

h) the plans are implemented;

i) the cycle is repeated as new needs are identified and further action or research is required.

This cycle has three basic components — research to provide data on particular needs or problems; discussion of the data; action which leads to further research and feedback. In this way key decision makers and their subordinates become more aware of their problems and hence, any new directions they may wish to take become that much clearer.

Full time commercial consultants, on the other hand, play a more limited role than the intermittent consultants, for they are hired to apply a packaged solution. The full time consultant markets himself as an expert in the use of certain techniques and therefore is hired to apply that technique. Further, full time consultancy is expensive and as time for consultancy is limited, the client would usually demand an observable result for his expenditure. Over a short time period, it is unreasonable to expect a consultant to become sensitive to the culture of the particular organisation. Consequently, it is unrealistic to expect a tailor-made solution to accommodate the problems at hand.

Consultants, advisors, specialist officers and facilitators, play a vital role in any organisation. Through them, issues that would not otherwise be faced, can be confronted, with the hope of working towards an acceptable solution. However, the use of third parties can be problematic. Their role is difficult to define and other members of the organisation may not be able to understand how to best use them. In order to best utilise a third party, managers must want to change or at least understand the processes taking place in their organisation.

Currently, the trend in SSDs is to reduce the number of persons in consultant type roles as their work and function are not well understood. Should this trend continue, then the number of people available to work on organisation design and re-design problems, will be severely limited.

Further re-organisation or integration?

In the discussions we have held with social services personnel, the question of whether further re-organisation is necessary, has arisen. Few people have been explicit as to why further re-organisation is required, but many have shared a common feeling that something additional needs to be done.

What factors within an organisation should be considered for re-organisation? Figure 4.1 indicates the four basic factors that would have to be considered in planning to re-organise any part of, or whole organisation.

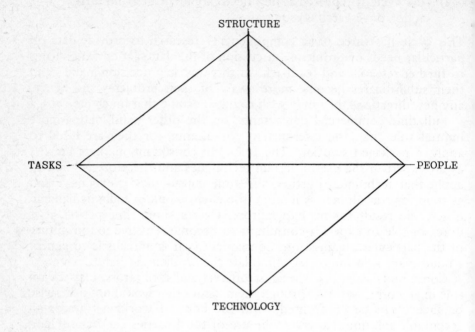

Figure 4.1   Four factors influencing the design of SSDs

If re-organisation is to take place, it will have to concentrate on one or more of the four factors identified in Figure 4.1, which will inevitably produce changes in the other three (see Table 4.4). At the time of re-organisation in 1970 and 1973/4, greatest emphasis was placed on the structure of SSDs. Considerable effort went into examining the required authority relationships within the hierarchy; role and functional definitions; the formal procedures and formal communication systems. Little attention was paid to tasks and virtually none to the technology of social work and the people who were to work within SSDs.

Consequently, if another re-organisation is to take place, what lines could it follow and for what reasons? Is there sufficient knowledge about the technology of social work to merit re-organisation? How much is known about the attitudes, norms and work practises of social services personnel operating at different levels in the hierarchy?

Table 4.4

Aspects of the four organisational factors

Structure

Re-organisation of authority relationships
Re-definition of roles
Re-consideration of formal procedures
Re-examination of the communication systems (e.g. committee structure)
Re-examination of the reward systems (payment methods and salary grades)

Technology

Re-examination of workflow systems
Re-examination of factors of technology
Re-consideration of decision making systems
Re-consideration of information systems and reporting mechanisms

People

Re-examination of selection procedures
Re-examination of training and education procedures
Re-examination of career development procedures
Re-consideration of counselling and consultative facilities

Tasks

Re-definition of tasks
Re-consideration of the need for job enrichment
Re-examination of supervisory procedures

Is in fact, so little known about people, technology and tasks that another re-organisation would only concentrate on the structure dimension and hence perpetuate problems that currently exist? In the end would another re-organisation provide no solution whatsoever?

Whether re-organisation is required or not; it is important to realise that after every major organisational change programme, it is necessary to enter into a phase of planned integration. Planned integration is the process of matching tasks, people, technology, cultures and structures with each other, so that the organisation can identify and work towards its mission and purpose.

The evidence of our research studies and the findings of others (Smith 1977; Mott 1977) indicates that effective planned integration has not taken place in SSDs. For example, just what is involved in the practise of social work? It was suggested in previous sections, that social work is really an individual's collection of subjective experiences and meanings which depending on the sensitivity and awareness of the

147

individual, will determine his actions with each client. How have social services integrated their technology and structure? The evidence in Parlsoe's and Stephenson's work and in my studies, strongly suggests that the technology of social work and the structure of SSDs are not well aligned. The development of creative task oriented groups with a vocational orientation towards 'person therapy' is unlikely to flourish within the current structures. In fact, Parlsoe and Stephenson indicate that 'practical help' as opposed to 'casework therapy' is the more popular service in most SSDs. It is no accident that providing clothes, goods, the offer of residential accommodation (i.e. things) is recognised as more valuable than more intensively oriented casework. The hierarchical structure of SSDs facilitates the provision of easily recognisable goods and services but not professional casework development.

The section in this chapter, on 'Professional satellite teams', constantly emphasised that an alternative structure is necessary if such teams are to flourish. Hence, the true purpose of the teams and the best way to organise the teams to achieve their purpose, are two prime considerations. These two 'prime considerations' are integration/ design/issues and not issues of re-organisation.

Each SSD will have to consider how best to arrange each of the four organisational factors — structure, people, technology and tasks in order to achieve their departmental objectives.

Below are certain issues that have to be considered if planned integration is to be achieved.

1 Planning
   The structure — centralisation/decentralisation.
   Co-ordination of activities.
   Monitoring standards of work.
   Developing an overall corporate strategy.
   Developing effective information systems.
   Identifying structure cross-over points.
   Innovative budgeting for the future.
2 Creativity
   Allowing for innovation by offering individuals freedom to meet and discuss.
   Developing new services.
   Identifying new needs.
   Planning effective change.
   Greater emphasis on collaboration than authority relationships.
3 Performance
   Creating new types of project teams.
   Greater emphasis on lateral as opposed to line relationships.
   Integrating professional services.

Making greater use of internal and external consultants.
Early warning systems for intra and inter-departmental problems.
Team building.
Senior management awareness of the different cultures operating within the organisation.

Summary

The design of SSDs requires the constant attention of senior management. From the results of the research studies in Part I, five areas of organisational design are identified.

First, it is important to decide whether to adopt a centralised or decentralised system. Arguments in favour of both policies are presented, indicating that centralisation provides for greater uniformity whereas decentralisation allows for diversity. Yet, simply to centralise or decentralise will not overcome organisational problems. Whichever policy is adopted, it is important to recognise that some form of human relations training should accompany the change programme, as working within different organisation structures requires a change of attitude and work behaviour on the part of those involved.

Probably, the most influential culture within SSDs is the role culture. Managers that operate within the role culture, control the administration of procedures, rules, regulations and information flows within each SSD. Consequently, it is recommended that an effective management information system (MIS) be installed, which would draw on information from fieldworkers and used as data for planning future policies and strategies.

Although an effective MIS will be useful to middle and senior managers, it is of little help in improving casework practise. In fact, evidence is produced to show that casework could be far more effective in a different organisational setting. If professional social work is to flourish, multi-disciplinary professional satellite teams need to be created, staffed by full time permanent and seconded personnel, who are qualified as doctors, nurses, police, social workers, community nurses etc. The purpose of these teams is to provide intensive and long-term casework for clients who face substantial problems. Such clients would be referred to the professional teams from SSDs, hospitals and police authorities. Two important features distinguish the teams from the parent organisation; the hierarchy is shallow so that all the team members are fieldwork practitioners; the teams are independently run and managed and only financed by the parent organisation which may be the SSD or area health authority.

Most large organisations need to use internal consultants and SSDs are no exception. However, the role of internal consultants in SSDs is poorly understood. Two case studies are presented to show that if consultants are not available or badly utilised, then potentially problematic situations can deteriorate to become major concerns. The value of consultants should be recognised and greater use made of internal and external consultants.

It is sometimes difficult to establish whether re-organisation or integration is the policy to follow. However, after any major re-organisation, a well thought through policy of integration is required. Whether re-organisation concentrates on organisation structure, technology, tasks or people, the remaining three factors have to be integrated with the fourth that was substantially changed. Probably, the planned integration of structure, technology tasks and people has not taken place in most SSDs.

5 Integrating the person with the organisation

Integrating people and their activities with the mission and objectives of the organisation is difficult. Most senior managers in public service and industrial organisations will have experienced the problem of persuading individuals, heads of units and departments, to make a genuine effort to tailor their activities in order to fit with organisational objectives.

As we have already seen, the size of the total organisation has a direct influence on the degree of integration that is possible within the organisation. In a smaller organisation, whatever the internal strains and stresses, cohesion is easier to achieve as group members can place considerable pressure on particular individuals who maybe considered deviant. In a larger organisation, the system of informal integration and control breaks down and is substituted by formal mechanisms. The larger the total collective becomes, the greater the need to break down into unit sizes that are manageable, both in terms of supervision of people and the allocation of tasks, and hence, the greater the need of formal procedures and rules to regulate the activities of numerous units. Establishing rules purely for the sake of control only will not do. Unless personnel within the department can identify with the rules that are instituted, then developing formal procedures will turn out to be a meaningless activity. Procedures, rules and regulations and in fact, all means of formal communication are important factors as far as the design of the organisation is concerned. The process of integrating the individual with the organisation is partly a problem of design in that integration will not occur unless certain design features have been attended to. However, an additional intervention is then required.

Let us assume that a social service department has been so designed to effectively face up to its internal difficulties and meet problems in the community. The fact that a system has been established within the department is only half the story. The other half is knowing how to manage the personnel in the department, who make the system work.

Ever since re-organisation in 1970, the process of managing the social services has been identified, in the literature, in terms of organisation structure, organisation roles and the tasks that each person in a particular role has to undertake. As indicated in the section 'Further re-organisation or integration', chapter 4, there is so much more to managing an organisation.

French and Bell (1978) put forward a useful idea; that of the organisational iceberg. Making organisational life synonymous with an iceberg is an interesting idea, for French and Bell identify that certain aspects of managing an organisation are overt and visible and certain aspects are covert and hidden. Figure 5.1 identifies both the overt and covert aspects of the organisational iceberg. The overt aspects of organisational life are the structures, policies, procedures and financial resources of the organisation. However, these are the top of the iceberg. The covert side remains hidden and is often not considered as part of managerial policy and practise. The covert side involves the perceptions, attitudes, feelings, values of individuals and group norms that result when certain individuals act towards common objectives. Effective managers will consider structure, policies and procedures simultaneously with understanding the perceptions of subordinates, their attitudes and feelings, and the values and norms of their peer group. Hence, two questions have to be answered if both the overt and covert aspects of organisational life are to be integrated: what problems can be identified and what steps can be taken to overcome these problems?

Spotting the problem

A problem that was identified by a number of the participants in the research programme is the lack of planned management development and training in SSDs. One area officer I interviewed stated:

> We have a number of problems in social services, the worst of which is that people in my position and more senior to me do not even recognise that they should be acting as managers. Second, the level of managerial skill is low amongst senior personnel in the social services, but can you blame them for they do not recognise the true nature of their work, which is management.

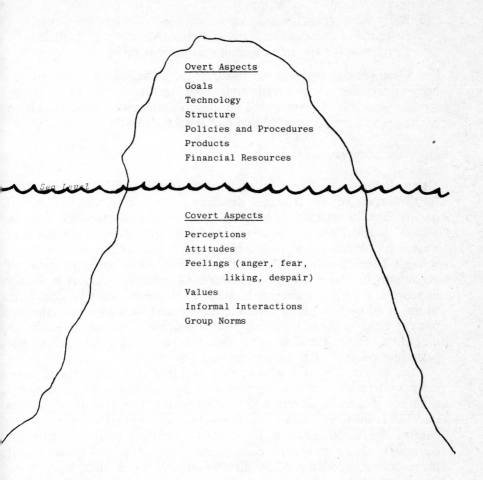

Overt Aspects

Goals
Technology
Structure
Policies and Procedures
Products
Financial Resources

Sea Level

Covert Aspects

Perceptions
Attitudes
Feelings (anger, fear,
          liking, despair)
Values
Informal Interactions
Group Norms

Source: French and Bell (1978) p. 16

Figure 5.1   Organisational iceberg

Three reasons are identified for the lack of management development. These are:

1 Greatest attention has been given to organisation structures.
2 Most managers in SSDs consider themselves as professional social work specialists and hence, greater emphasis has been given to social work training.
3 SSDs have only been in existence for ten years in Great Britain and consequently, the skills necessary to managerially problem solve are only beginning to be recognised.

For these reasons little or no research on management problems has been undertaken in the social services, or for that matter, in the public services generally. However, the studies in Part I give a good indication of the problems managers have to face in today's SSDs.

Problems identified in research

Three distinctly different cultures have been identified within SSDs. As the career of any manager develops, he will find that his job will involve him in relating to people from all three cultures. He must be able to diagnose the problems and then put into practise a management style with which he is comfortable and is also effective in problem solving. Theoretically, he should be sufficiently flexible in his style and behaviour to cover all three cultures. Practically, that is probably impossible for most managers to achieve. However, what he does have to do, is accurately identify problem areas and then assess whether his present style is suited to solving those particular problems. Table 5.1 identifies certain problem symptoms that emanate from each of the particular cultures identified in the research studies.

1 Task culture. Persons who operate within a task culture tend to be more concerned with solving problems by utilising their professional skills and expertise, as opposed to establishing rules and procedures as possible contingency strategies. Consequently, trying to systematically control the activities of task oriented specialists is always difficult. At worst, the response to control can become pathological in that management is confronted by direct hostility. When social workers no longer adhere to rules, are hostile towards management, do not trust the intentions of management and do not identify with the organisation, then the situation requires immediate attention. In situations where task oriented professionals reject management outright, problems such as poor work performance standards, poor team identity, irregular attendance at work and poor motivation to develop new activities, will become common place.

2 Role culture. In order to perform effectively within a role culture, people have to accept the pattern of pre-determined roles, rules and

Table 5.1

Problem symptoms

Task culture	Role culture	Power culture
No adherence to rules	Over control	Unable to think strategically
Hostility towards management	Over administration	Unable to facilitate relationships
Poor performance standards	Over punitive	Unable to accurately time actions and policies
Low trust	Inability to understand 'true' needs of outsiders	Unable to cope with ambiguity
Poor team identity	Resent outsiders for up-setting the status quo	Unable to cope with stress
No organisational identity		
Irregular attendance at work		
Poor motivation to do new things		

procedures. When people do not adhere to the pattern of rules and regulations, managers within the role culture could react by introducing a greater number of controls and generally behaving punitively towards those that are seen to break rules and regulations.

Procedures and rules are established, not only to control situations but further to cover all possible contingencies. This is in direct contrast to the manner of operation of task culture oriented specialists. Social workers who are responsible for particularly problematic cases need to discuss with their colleagues what action should be taken next. They do not need to refer to procedures to give them guidance and direction. The problem is that of flexibility, for by not being sufficiently flexible to meet new and unforeseen eventualities, managers operating within a role culture will find it difficult to understand the 'true' needs of persons outside the role culture. Any outsiders, whether they be clients, social workers or elected representatives will be resented for upsetting the status quo. In fact, in the interviews I conducted, elected representatives were identified by middle managers as a major problem. One area officer stated:

> Councillors are a problem because they do not understand what we are doing. They think they can walk in here and

just change everything just because they have become involved in a case. Half the problem is that they just do this for political gain and are not really interested in what we do. Whenever a councillor comes here demanding action, I just let him shout his mouth off, pretend I am going to do something and then do nothing.

The statement by the area officer is more extreme than most, but the general opinion that elected representatives do not positively wish to help was commonly held. In order to obtain a balanced picture, I spoke to the councillor to whom the area officer was referring. He stated:

I sometimes have a hell of a job with this department. The basic problem is that they resent me coming in to ask questions about people who have problems and live in my constituency. There is no political gain for me just because I become involved in a case. However, if something goes drastically wrong with that case, then we all lose; me and the social services people. It is a pity that we cannot co-operate better.

Whatever the true intentions of the local authority councillor, one thing is certain, the particular SSD in question, could not harness his skills towards providing a service to the community.

3 Power culture. To become a success in a power culture it is simply necessary to become powerful. Individuals with such ambitions have to develop the skills of persuasion and facilitation. In addition person oriented skills have to be coupled with the cognitive skill of understanding and developing long-term strategies. Strategies and policies are the key around which all other activities depend. Once the objectives that the organisation can realistically pursue have been established, then systems and procedures can be identified that can operationalise longer term strategies into shorter term work objectives, which can in turn be acted upon in terms of tasks.

Identifying future strategies is a creative activity and as with most creative work, it is riddled with ambiguity. If an individual cannot tolerate ambiguity, he will experience stress. Experiencing stress will reduce his potential for creativity, his sense of timing in knowing when it is most appropriate to introduce particular actions and policies for consideration and even his ability to facilitate social relationships. Senior managers who continue to operate in situations stressful to them, will perform poorly. Eventually, morale and trust throughout the organisation will become low.

Problem solving steps

Based on the data gathered in Part I, six problem solving steps have been identified (Figure 5.2):

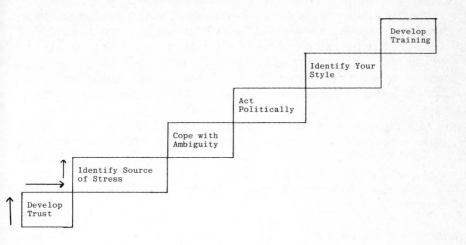

Figure 5.2   Problem solving steps

Develop trust

Most managers face a constant problem; on the one hand they are held accountable for the activities of others and hence have to maintain control; on the other, they need to delegate certain activities to their subordinates. Practically, it means developing a sense of trust in the competence of your subordinate.

The greater majority of managers in SSDs operate within a role culture setting, at the middle of the organisation. For a middle manager, the easier reaction to any problem would be to impose control. However, there is always the danger that the imposition of control will lead to defensive reaction and a resistance to control. The dilemma of the manager is how to balance trust and control. Practically speaking, trust, from the middle managers point of view could well imply allowing someone the luxury of making a mistake.

The situation is not simple, for the middle manager in turn is held accountable by his manager for any mistakes that occur. Consequently, the question of whether to impose greater control or allow greater personal freedom over work activities is not simply a personal decision. The decision to develop trust or impose control is dependent on the bosses boss. Consequently, the style of the director and his team is crucial for they will set the pattern to which middle management will respond.

It is generally accepted by behavioural scientists that the more successful organisation places greater emphasis on trust than control. Trust is shared by all members of the organisation in that they accept greater personal responsibility for their actions. If things are going well, it is easier to relinquish control, for shared responsibility, trust and participation are seen as contributing to the success of the organisation.

Although many behavioural scientists would like to think that the trust − success cycle begins with trust, it is probably more realistic to assume that success has led to trust and participation and not the other way round. A middle manager therefore, must have confidence that if he adopts a policy of participation and trust, then success will be the outcome.

Some SSDs have begun participation schemes, but in reality most of the issues discussed are unimportant to the continued development of the organisation. Participants in such participation schemes have become frustrated by their low level of influence and rather than trust increasing, it has decreased and conflict oriented relationships have developed. Any manager that works to increase the level of trust in his unit or section will have to experiment, but there are certain strategies he can adopt to improve his chances of success:

1 Develop relationships with team leaders. It is crucial that middle managers develop a good relationship with team leaders. Senior social workers are the group who have to manage the boundary between the task and role cultures. Should they become suspicious that the intentions of middle management are not 'honest', then the trusting relationship between the team leader and middle manager will be poor. A good working relationship between the two is necessary, for team leaders have the power to block the development of any new ideas within the teams by ensuring that only the minimum is done.

2 Team building. Team building is a useful technique for breaking down unfavourable stereotypes that individuals or groups hold of each other. Most managers have probably experienced situations where their group or team views them with suspicion. Communication between the manager and his team decreases, personal relations deteriorate and scoring 'political' points off each other becomes more important than solving common problems. A poor relationship between two groups or between the group and its manager, can easily reach a win/lose situation. Team building is a way of openly confronting differences

158

between groups and people within groups. Various methods of team building exist;

a) holding human relations workshops whereby the conflicting parties openly discuss their difficulties;

b) establishing a task force made up of people who openly have difficulties with each other. The aim of the group is to work together to achieve certain practical task objectives such as identifying ways of meeting particular community problems. People who found it difficult to co-operate with each other in the past, are put into a team setting to achieve practical objectives within a limited time period and thereby have to re-examine their previous style of work practice.

Realistically, team work cannot be expected to thrive in some departments. Certain SSDs do have a mismatch between structural and cultural conditions. Team building can only work when the organisation is so designed that team development can realistically be expected to flourish. If the formal structure makes no allowance for the need to work together, then goodwill between people, which is the basis of team building, will not develop.

3 Use third parties. The value of third party consultants has already been discussed in chapter 4. Suffice it to say that an effective third party consultant is the bridge between persons who hold different personal values and objectives, and between groups and individuals whose relationships have deteriorated. In situations where relationships are poor, the intervention of a third party is required in order to stimulate meaningful discussion between people. Depending on the situation, the discussion can be conducted within a group setting by the consultant, or on a more individual counselling basis. Whatever the style of the intervention, the third party acts as the catalyst, helping people change their present pattern of work practise but on their terms and in their way.

4 Stimulate professional development. The research studies in Part I indicate that managers more than social workers, attended professional conferences. Consequently, greater attention should be given to the professional development of social workers by financing their attendance at conferences and seminars. The conference provides a forum for discussion, where problems that are faced by personnel in SSDs can be raised and thrashed out. However, few professional social work organisations have considered it necessary to hold conferences on the theme of 'Managing the Social Services'. Greater attention should be paid, as part of the professional development of SSD personnel, to the organisational problems of social work.

The study of stress at work has recently become popular within industrial organisations but as yet has not been examined in public service organisations. Consequently, managers in SSDs, or any other local authority department, may not be able to recognise the symptoms of stress when they occur within themselves or colleagues. Being able to identify the symptoms and sources of stress is an important first step. Cooper (1979) identifies several sources of stress.

1 Factors intrinsic to the job are an important source of stress. Stress can be caused by too much or too little work, time pressures and deadlines, too many decisions to make in conflicting circumstances, fatigue from physical strains, having to cope with too many changes at work and having to face mistakes made by oneself or subordinates. The studies in chapter 3 indicate that team leaders and assistant directors may be especially prone to stress. Both the team leader and the assistant director have to work in situations of ambiguity and contradiction; namely they have to manage the demands of people who work within a task culture and role culture, and a role culture and power culture respectively. From studies in industry, the personality and motivational characteristics of team leaders and senior managers are important considerations in terms of stress. For example, personality and motivational characteristics are factors as extrovert or introvert; flexible or rigid; inner or outer directed; open or close minded; achievement/ status or security oriented. The studies in industry indicate that outer-directed people are more adaptable and more highly reality oriented than inner-directed persons; achievement seekers show more independence and job involvement than security seekers etc. It is important for each individual to realise his personal needs and personality characteristics and relate these to his performance and the role ambiguity that he has to tolerate in doing his job.

2 Relations within the organisation have been identified as a potential source of stress. Poor relations and personality conflicts with superiors, subordinates and colleagues makes it difficult to call on others to help solve problems or delegate responsibility. Possibly, senior managers may not recognise how stressful certain problems brought to their attention can be for their subordinate. The problems may be considered trivial, petty or time consuming and therefore any requests for action from those below, will not be recognised as a genuine demand.

3 Career development, or the lack of it is a constant source of stress and frustration. It is probably, a commonly held image that only those who are 'achievement oriented' will succeed in management. For SSDs in 1970, such an image was reality, for re-organisation created a large number of senior positions that had previously not existed, but needed to be filled. Ten years on, we have or will have two career development problems in SSDs:

a) people who were over-promoted, due to re-organisation;
b) the disillusioned young and middle-aged who are under promoted and face few prospects of further development.

People who are over-promoted are those that cannot fully comprehend the true nature of the demands made on them by others, what their job entails and the fact that their ability to think strategically is limited. Consequently, over-promoted managers tend to view their work on a short-term basis, are unable to devise plans for the future and respond to ambiguous demands or criticism by scapegoating or over-controlling the activities of other people. Equally, under-promoted managers have to face the frustration of feeling trapped and being subordinate to managers whom they consider less able than themselves. Problems of career frustration, lack of commitment and lack of respect for superiors can partly be overcome by developing greater trust amongst individuals and groups within the hierarchy.

4 Structure/culture interface is an important characteristic that has been emphasised throughout this book. The larger the organisation, the greater the likelihood of the restrictions over consultation, communication and participation in decision making. Equally, the greater the likelihood of formal controls imposed upon individuals and groups in the organisation. Consequently, if SSDs are not to become highly centralised/formalised organisations, the organisation has to be so designed to accommodate the technology, tasks, people and structure, so that its mission and objectives can be achieved.

5 Work/home interface. Inevitably, stress experienced at work will begin to show itself in the home life. The little research carried out in this area indicates that most young managers seem to fight to maintain a distance between the wife and the organisation, so that she is not in a position to evaluate the choices he has to make. Paradoxically, he does this at a time when he needs most support and understanding. The other stress factors that have a bearing on home life are working late, paying too much attention to the job and not enough to the family and generally being unable to use the wife as a counsellor. Recent studies by Margerison (1980) in industrial organisations and by myself in local authority departments shows that a poor work/home interface is viewed as most stressful by middle managers.

Any individual that experiences stress will adopt certain behaviours as a direct reaction. The behaviours could be adaptive or maladaptive. Taking some of the stress symptoms described above, certain possible adaptive and maladaptive reactions are shown in Table 5.2.

Most individuals will have experienced maladaptive behaviour. A certain amount of patience and understanding from colleagues, superiors and subordinates will help an individual change maladaptive behaviour to adaptive behaviour. It is important therefore, to be able

161

Table 5.2

Adaptive and maladaptive reactions to stress

Area of stress	Adaptive behaviour	Maladaptive behaviour
Overworked	Delegate work	Accepts overload and performance deteriorates
Unaware of SSD policy	Find out nature of policy	Guesses incorrectly and performs inappropriately
Poor working relationships	Confront issues with others	Attacks others indirectly
Underpromoted	Leave	Loses confidence
Work/home interface	Take a holiday	Blames family or department or both
Role ambiguity	Clarify role with superiors	Withdraws from certain aspects of work

(Adapted from Cooper 1979 p. 163/164).

to identify maladaptive behaviour.

Cope with ambiguity

Senior management is continuously faced with the problem of identifying and resolving dilemmas. The dilemmas could concern reconciling departmental objectives with the differing objectives of different groups in the organisation; coping with the different leadership styles of managers, and trade unionists and reconciling the needs of professional personnel with departmental requirements. Hence, the objectives that senior management wishes to achieve have to be realistic according to the organisational context from which they operate. No one person will ever be certain that he is 'doing the right thing'. Successful senior managers are ones that:

a) identify the dilemmas faced by the organisation;
b) are able to discuss with individuals or groups the disparate demands made and can develop a plan to reconcile those demands;
c) can put a strategic plan into operation even in the face of opposition.

The ability of any senior manager to cope with ambiguity involves not only identifying new strategies for the future but facing up to the difficulties of operationalising those strategies. The process is difficult, especially if a choice has to be made between two well founded and competently presented but irreconcilable arguments, put forward by two competing individuals or groups. Reconciling strategy formulation and strategy implementation places pressure on senior managers which they not only have to survive but further, turn into success.

Act politically

The formulation and implementation of strategy involves making choices between alternative courses of action. Where disparate demands are made, any decision that is reached is 'political'. Certain parties will feel aggrieved that their demands were not met. The manager has to somehow accommodate their grievances, for the same group have to continue with their task activities but without any drop in performance standards. Acting 'politically' involves harnessing sufficient force to implement policy decisions that were made in the face of conflicting demands and yet ensure that the organisation continues functioning. How does a manager act?

Four strategies of political action are identified:
1 Affiliation. The ability to 'get on' with other people is an important aspect of management activity. Whether discussing informally or negotiating formally, it is vital that the other party feels they can approach management on most issues. Consequently, every manager needs to realise that his personal style should suit the occasion. However stressful and distasteful the negotiation may be, maintaining an open channel of communication with other parties is vital.
2 Withholding and withdrawing. It is impossible to satisfy the needs of all parties in a large, diverse organisation. One way of ensuring that certain groups do not 'over-react' to issues which they recognise as important, is to withhold information. By preventing certain information from becoming common knowledge, the manager is able to achieve whatever objectives he has identified without facing opposition that could destroy his plan. In such circumstances, management should be fairly convinced that its plan is valuable. It is just that others have not yet recognised its worth. To constantly withhold information is not recommended, for such behaviour is indicative of a manager who cannot confront certain problems. Continuously withholding information is a means of protecting the manager and not the policy.

Withdrawing from a situation is also vital. There are times when the presence of management in a dispute or negotiation, is of no help. To withdraw and allow the different factions to negotiate their own terms, or for management to withdraw an unpopular policy and shelve it for the time being, are common practises. The larger and more diverse an organisation becomes, the more important is the timing of actions. When to introduce or withdraw plans and information are important considerations for policy implementation.

3 Exchange, or the ability to 'make a deal' with other individuals or groups, is common practise in most large organisations. Where resources are scarce, different individuals or groups will agree to support each other to achieve a common purpose as long as there are benefits for them. The way 'deals' are made, is as important as the actual 'deal' itself. In more hierarchically oriented organisations, there is a greater likelihood that groups at the lower levels of the organisation will combine resources in opposition to senior management. Senior managements response would be to impose greater rules and regulations in order to recapture control. Within a more decentralised, matrix type structure, the opposite is true, namely that making deals with groups from different organisational levels is a common experience. Whether the organisation is centralised or matrix oriented, the larger it becomes the greater is the likely incidence of agreements made between management and particular groups. The fact that some individual agreements are realised and others not, is not indicative of an unhealthy organisation. It is a sign of attempting to accommodate the genuine but different needs of different operational units.

4 Presentation. The ability to present an argument coherently is an important skill for senior managers. In a recent study I conducted, examining how senior managers in local authorities make decisions, it became clear that the more 'successful' directors of departments were the ones who dominated the chief officers management team meetings. Dominating the chief officers meetings involved arguing clearly and also being able to control the flow of conversation between individuals at the meeting. Less 'successful' chief officers were ones who held equally competent ideas but found it difficult to justify them verbally. Consequently, their ideas were dismissed with greater ease even though they may have been valuable. Over a period of time, those who could argue forcefully were generally looked upon as the informal leaders of the chief officers team. Their policies and ideas tended to be adopted more than those of others. In one authority, especially, the key to success was the ability to present a favourable public image and control conversations within groups.

Identify your style

In the research studies we conducted, I interviewed and observed three effective, but quite different assistant directors. The individual style and approach to problem spotting and problem solving of each assistant director is presented in Table 5.3.

Assistant director 1 was more open, approachable, honest, confront-

Table 5.3

Three assistant directors — problem solving and problem spotting

Assistant director 1	Assistant director 2	Assistant director 3
Works well in a group setting	Does not require the presence of others	Does not work well in group settings
Others feel able to contact her and discuss personal and work problems with her	Others feel able to contact him for guidance, approval or disapproval over work issues	Others only approach him for a decision on their work
Confronts issues directly and states where she stands in negotiations	Makes sure he wins in all negotiations	Offers little or no information when negotiating
Is always searching for new potential in situations and people	Looks for potential to make current situation work better	Ensures that others stay within the established pattern of rules and regulations
Pays no attention to her own or others rank and seniority	Uses his authority readily but pays no heed to the authority and status of others	Uses his authority readily but pays great attention to the rank and status of others

ing and paid little attention to the organisational position she or others held. Equally effective was assistant director 2 whose main objective was to succeed in whatever he attempted. He preferred to work on his own so that he could orient himself to his personal success. However, when he had to work with others, he ensured that they worked towards obtaining his objectives. Assistant director 2 is not an innovator, for thinking about new ways of doing things and actually doing them will involve taking risks and risks may lead to failure. Assistant director 3 worked well when he interacted least with other people. The primary objective of assistant director 3 was to make the existing pattern of rules and regulations work as effectively as possible. As long as others understood their expected role, he could see little need for interaction. However, assistant director 3 was a competent negotiator, fully aware of the procedures, regulations and constraints within the department, a knowledge which he used in most bargaining situations.

Each of the three assistant directors is capable and competent, but each with different managerial styles. The department that employed them was able to tolerate the three distinctly different styles of the senior managers. Assistant director 1 had a good relationship with social workers and team leaders. She fitted in well with those working within a task culture. Assistant director 2 was ambitious and only worked towards his next appointment, which he hoped would be that of a director. He functioned well in a power culture. Assistant director 3 was a competent administrator, ensuring that the present system of rules and regulations worked well. Yet, assistant director 3 lacked flair and innovation. Although assistant director 3 was a well respected senior administrator, most of his colleagues recognised that he had reached the top of his career. He operated best in a role culture.

Based on Harrison's four cultural types, Table 5.4 indicates some stereotypic characteristics required of an individual to fit effectively in each culture. Most people will recognise that they 'fit' into one or possibly two cultural settings, such as operating successfully within a role culture but also feeling comfortable within a power culture. However, persons who hold a preference for working within task or person oriented cultures will experience difficulty in identifying within role or power cultures. I have heard senior managers in SSDs criticised that in the early stages of their career, they were not competent social workers. The way SSDs are currently structured, they need not be, or have been, competent field workers.

Table 5.4

Managerial styles and organisational preferences

Role	Task
Certainty	Goals
Roles	Clients
Controls	Feedback
Hierarchical	Adaptable
Practical	Professional

Power	Person
Policies/strategies	Leaderless
Culture	Humanitarian
Communication	Flexible
Self	Idealistic
Clarity	Decentralised

Training

Training in social work currently encompasses two major areas:

a) professional training;
b) conferences, seminars, short courses, etc.

Professional training is available at polytechnics and universities on a full time and part time basis for one or two years duration. Short courses and conferences are organised by professional societies such as BASW or CCSWT. The two major topics that are always missing from any social work training programme, are organisation and management development.

Understanding the influence the organisation has on individuals and how best to develop managers within SSDs, goes unrecognised as an important area of study. Why enter into organisational type training? The purpose of organisationally related training is to help employees of all levels understand the key criteria that determine their behaviour at work. From understanding why people adopt certain attitudes and practise certain behaviours, decisions can be reached as to whether the department's structure and managerial styles are conducive to the practise of social work. The aim of training is to help the personnel within the organisation more effectively achieve their work objective.

Most management development programmes are a form of human relations training. Three types of human relations training programmes are identified.

1 Small group training – aimed at increasing self-awareness for individuals. The objective is to help the participants understand why they behave and react the way they do. Traditionally, encounter groups and T-groups have been the more popular form of small group programmes. The groups are usually unstructured in nature with the participants organising their own programme through discussing and analysing issues that are pertinent to them.

2 Structured programme training – has become more popular in recent years. Again, this form of training is based on small group work, but the participants are asked to attend courses or workshops which have a central theme such as leadership, identifying managerial styles, improving negotiating skills, improving supervisory skills, or improving decision making skills. Both unstructured awareness group training and structured programme training, involve participants learning about themselves and their work environment.

3 Practical problem solving project groups – project group training is a form of group sensitivity and personal development training, but with the objective that the project group works towards solving particular problems that are currently faced by the organisation. Project group training has by its very nature an on-the-job philosophy. Participants are taken away from their immediate job pressures and are asked to examine why certain organisational problems have arisen and what realistic solutions can be applied to overcome the problems. As the term states, project work involves meeting certain objectives, but using the process of problem solving to develop the skills of the project group participants in human interaction.

All three forms of human relations training are dependent on competent group leaders. Usually, most organisations do not have staff who are capable of organising and running these types of programmes. Hence, an outsider whether employed by a business school or private consultancy organisation, is hired to run programmes. Hiring outsiders can be expensive, which may explain why SSDs have not ventured into this field.

One outcome of successful training programmes is that the participants will become less organisationally dependent. On examining their personal needs and behaviour, people may well conclude that they expected too much from their place of employment. However, senior management may not be able to cope with people who are more independent. From this point of view, any form of human relations training may be considered unacceptable. Ideally, senior managers should be first to experience management development training in order to be prepared for changes in the style of their subordinates, after they have experienced training.

How do subordinates react to the new manager recently returned from training? If the manager decides that a more participative style is in order, then he should prepare his subordinates for the change of style. It is difficult for others to respond positively to a person who previously adopted an authoritarian stance, but is now more participative.

Above all, it is necessary to identify why training is necessary, Management training makes people aware of themselves, others and the structures that surround them. Unless some re-design of the organisation is to take place, human relations training, from senior management's point of view, could be more of a hindrance than help. Course participants will not return from the programme and easily settle to their old pattern of behaviour. If, on the other hand, senior management is considering re-designing and re-structuring their department, part of their policy should be to build in some form of training. Changing the structure without an examination of previously held attitudes and behaviour, will mean that, in reality, no change takes place.

Summary

Research has identified a number of problems that personnel in SSDs will have to face. Certain problems will require considering issues of organisational design. Other problems have to be examined under the umbrella of interpersonal skills. Six areas of interpersonal skills are worthy of further analysis.

The need to develop a trusting relationship between persons who identify with different organisational cultures, is of vital importance. The relationship between team leaders and middle managers is crucial as team leaders provide the gatekeeper role between the task and role cultures. In addition to holding structured team building programmes, the availability of third party consultation is recommended, as part of a programme of organisational integration.

Stress is a likely problem that both fieldworkers and managers in SSDs are currently experiencing. Hence, being able to identify the sources of stress, is an important step to overcoming stress.

As SSDs are large, diverse organisations, identifying particular skills for managers to adopt in strategy implementation is necessary. In fact, it is recommended that managers should realise that they have to become 'politically' astute in the way they relate to individuals and groups, in the way they utilise information and reach agreements for future action.

With these constant pressures, the ability to cope with ambiguity and contradiction as part of every day organisational life is a skill that managers must develop. In order to develop their repetoire of skills, managers in SSDs should be able to identify their strengths in terms of their managerial style. Identifying one's style should not be left totally as the responsibility of the individual. The whole process of style identification, managerial training and developing an understanding of behaviour in organisations should be structured as planned management training programmes. If senior management wishes to realistically introduce change in their SSD, then both the design of the department and the attitudes and work behaviour of the personnel, have to be attended to.

Bibliography

Algie, J., (1970) 'Management and Organisation in the Social Services'. *British Hospital Journal and Social Service Review.* Vol. 80, pp. 1245-8.

Algie, J., (1973a) 'Merging Public Services'. *Management Decision.* Vol. II, Winter, pp. 280-293.

Algie, J., (1973b) 'Science for Social Welfare'. *Management Decision.* Vol. II, Spring, pp. 21-26.

Arbuckle, D.S., (1969) 'The Alienated Counsellor'. *Personnel and Guidance Journal.* Vol. 48, pp. 18-23.

Argris, C. and Schon, D.A., (1978) *Organisational Learning: A Theory of Action Perspective.* Addison-Wesley, Reading, Massachusetts.

Bains Report (1972) Study Group on Local Authority Management Structures. *The New Local Authority Management and Structures.* HMSO, London.

Baker, R.J.S., (1972) *'Administrative Theory and Public Administration'.* Hutchinson, London.

Barter, J., (1969) 'Management in Social Science'. *British Hospital Journal and Social Service Review.* Vol. 79, pp. 1220-1.

Belok, M.V., (1970) 'Teachers and Alienation', *Indian Journal of Social Research.* Vol. II, pp. 219-224.

Biller, R.P., (1971) 'Some Implications of Adaptation Capacity for Organisational and Political Development', in Marini, F. (ed). *Toward a New Public Administration: The Minnawbrook Perspective.* Scrauton, Chandler, pp. 92-121.

Bonjean, A.H. and Grimes, M.D., (1970) 'Bureaucracy and Alienation: A Dimensional Approach'. *Social Forces.* Vol. 49, pp. 622-630.

Brayfield, A.H. and Crockett, W.H., (1957) 'Employee Attitudes and Performance'. *Psychological Bulletin*. Vol. 52, pp. 307-318.

Buchanan, G., II (1975) 'Red-tape and the Service Ethic: some Unexpected Differences between Public and Private Managers'. *Administration and Society*. Vol. 6, pp. 423-444.

Carpenter, H.H., (1971) 'Formal Organisational Structural Factors and Perceived Job Satisfaction of Classroom Teachers'. *Administrative Science Quarterly*. Vol. 16, pp. 460-465.

Child, J., (1977) *Organisation: A Guide to Problems and Practise*. Harper & Row, London.

Cooper, C., (1979) *The Executive Gypsy*. Macmillan, London.

Cooper, C. and Marshal, J., (1978) *Understanding Executive Stress*. Macmillan, London.

Crozier, M., (1968) 'The Present Convergence of Public Administration and Large Private Enterprise and its Consequences'. *International Social Science Journal*. Vol. 20, pp. 7-16.

Etzioni, A., (1964) *Modern Organisations*. Prentice Hall, New York.

Etzioni, A., (1970) *Intervention Theory and Method: A Behavioural View*. Addison & Wesley, Massachusetts.

Falk, N. and Lee, J., (1978) *Planning the Social Services*. Saxon House, Teakfield, Hampshire.

French, W. and Bell, C.H., Jr. (1978) *Organisation Development: Behavioural Science Interventions for Organisation Improvement*. 2nd Ed. Prentice Hall, New York.

Garner, L., (1979) *The National Health Service: Your Money or Your Life*. Penguin, Harmondsworth.

Gaston, J., (1975) 'Autonomy in the Research Role and Participation in Departmental Decision Making'. *British Journal of Sociology*. Vol. XXVI, pp. 227-241.

Goldberg, E.M. and Fruin, D.J., (1976) 'Towards Accountability in Social Work: A Case Review System for Social Workers'. *British Journal of Social Work*. Vol. 6, pp. 3-22.

Goldberg, E.M., Warburton, R.W., Lyons, L.J., Willmott, R.R., (1978) 'Towards Accountability in Social Work: Long Term Social Work in an Area Office'. *British Journal of Social Work*. Vol. 8, Part 3, pp. 253-287.

Gowler, D. and Parry, G., (1979) 'Professionalism and its Discontent'. *The Journal of the Psychology and Psychotherapy Association*. Winter/Spring, pp. 54-56.

Green Paper, (1970) *National Health Service: The Future Structure of the NHS*. HMSO, London.

Green, S., (1975) 'Professional/Bureaucratic Conflict: The Case of the Medical Professional in the National Health Service'. *The Sociological Review*. Vol. 23, pp. 121-141.

Greenwood, A., (1965) 'The Attributes of a Profession', in Zald, M., (ed). *Social Welfare Institutions*. Wiley, New York, pp. 509-23.

Hackman, J.R., (1969) 'Nature of Tasks as a Determiner of Job Behaviour'. *Personnel Psychology*. Vol. 22, pp. 435-444.

Hage, J. and Aiken, M., (1967a) 'Programme Change and Organisational Properties'. *American Journal of Sociology*. Vol. 72, pp. 503-519.

Hage, J. and Aiken, M., (1967b) 'The Relationship of Centralisation to Other Structural Properties'. *Administrative Science Quarterly*. Vol. 12, pp. 73-92.

Hage, J. and Aiken, M., (1969) 'Routine Technology, Social Structure and Organisational Goals'. *Administrative Science Quarterly*. Vol. 14, pp. 366-375.

Handy, C.B., (1976) *Understanding Organisations*. Penguin, Harmondsworth.

Harrison, R., (1972) 'How to Describe Your Organisation'. *Harvard Business Review*. September-October 1972.

Hartmann, (1969) 'Anomie and Social Casework'. *Social Casework*. Vol. 50, pp. 131-137.

Hasenfeld, Y., (1972) 'People Processing Organisations: An Exchange Approach'. *American Sociological Review*. Vol. 37, June, pp. 256-263.

Hersch, C., (1966) 'Mental Health Services and The Poor'. *Psychiatry*. Vol. 29, pp. 236-245.

Hopkins, J., (1969) 'Social Work Organisations — New Models for Old'. *Case Conference*. Vol. 16, pp. 206-311.

Humes, C.W. and Kennedy, T.F., Jr. (1970) 'The Counsellor's Role in Collective Negotiations'. *Personnel and Guidance Journal*. Vol. 48, pp. 449-456.

Kahn, R.L., Wolfe, D.M., Quin, R.P. and Surek, J.D., (1964) *Organisational Stress: Studies in Role Conflict and Ambiguity*. Wiley, New York.

Kakabadse, A.P. and Warroll, R.M., (1978) 'Job Satisfaction and Organisation Structure: A Comparative Study of Nine Social Service Organisations'. *British Journal of Social Work*. Vol. 8, Part I, pp. 51-70.

Kingdon, D.R., (1973) *Matrix Organisation: Managing Information Technologies*, Tavistock, London.

Katz, D. and Kahn, R.L., (1966) *The Social Psychology of Organisations*. Wiley, New York.

Kogan, M., (1971) 'Management Efficiency and The Social Services: A Review Article'. *British Journal of Social Work*. Vol. 6, pp. 23-42.

Kogan, M., Cang, S., Dixon, M. and Tolliday, H., (1971) *Working Relationships within the British Hospital Service*. Bookstall Publications, London.

Kogan, M. and Terry, J., (1971) *The Organisation of a Social Service Department: A Blue Print*. Bookstall Publications, London.

Kohn, M.L., (1971) 'Bureaucratic Man: A Portrait and an Interpretation'. *American Sociological Review*. Vol. 36, pp. 461-478.

Mallaby Report, (1966) 'Committee on the Stopping of Local Government'. *Report on Local Government*. HMSO, London.

Maniha, J.K., (1974) 'The Standardisation of Elite Careers in Bureaucratising Organisations'. *Social Forces*. Vol. 53, pp. 282-288.

March, J.G. and Simon, A.A., (1958) *Organisations*. McGraw-Hill, New York.

Margerison, C.J., (1980) 'Leadership Paths and Profiles'. *Leadership and Organisation Development Journal*. Vol. No. 1, pp, 12-17.

Marran, B. and Buchanan, B., (1979) 'Changing Child Abuse'. *Community Care*. May 10, p. 14.

Maud Report, (1967) *Committee on the Management of Local Government*, Vol. 1, HMSO, London.

Meltzer, L. and Slater, J., (1962) 'Organisational Structure and the Performance and Job Satisfaction of Physiologists'. *American Sociological Review*. Vol. 27, No. 3, pp. 351-62.

Morgan, J.B., (1980) *Exeter Combined Police/Social Services Juvenile Bureau*. Paper presented to The International Conference on Strategies against Crimes in Europe. Cranfield Institute of Technology, Cranfield, Bedfordshire.

Morris, P., (1979) 'Child Abuse: What role for NSPCC?' *Community Care*. February 22nd, pp. 16-17.

Mott, J., (1977) 'Decision Making and Social Inquiry Reports in One Juvenile Court'. *British Journal of Social Work*. Vol. 7, No. 4, pp. 423-432.

Mumford, E., (1970) 'Job Satisfaction: A New Approach Derived from an Old Theory'. *Sociological Review*. Vol. 18, pp. 71-101.

Newman, A.D. and Rowbottom, R.W., (1968) *Organisation Analysis*. Heinemann, London.

Parsloe, P. and Stevenson, O., (1978) *Social Service Teams: The Practitioners View*. HMSO, London.

Payne, R., (1975) *Some Empirical and Conceptual Studies of Behaviour in Organisations*. Unpublished Ph.D. Thesis, London Graduate School of Business.

Payne, R.L. and Phesy, D.C., (1971) 'G.G. Stern's Organisational Climate Index: A Reconceptualisation and Application to Business Organisations'. *Organisation Behaviour and Human Performance*. Vol. 6, pp. 77-87.

Pritchard, R.D. and Karasick, B.W., (1973) 'The Effects of Organisational Climate on Managerial Job Performance and Job Satisfaction'. *Organisational Behaviour and Human Performance*.

Vol. 9, pp. 126-146.

Rowbottom, R.W. and Hey, A.M., (1973) Organising the Social Services — A Second Chance. *Local Government Chronicle.* No. 5526, pp. 127-131.

Rowbottom, R.W., Hey, A.M. and Billis, D., (1974) *Social Service Departments: Developing Patterns of Work and Organisation.* Heinemann, London.

Salmon Report, (1966) Report of the Committee on Senior Nursing Staff Structure. HMSO, London.

Schumacher, E.F., (1974) *Small Is Beautiful.* Abacus, London.

Seebohm Report, (1968) Report of the Committee on Local Authority and Allied Personal Social Services. HMSO, London.

Smith, G., (1977) 'Little Kiddies and Criminal Acts: The Role of Social Worker in the Children's Hearings'. *British Journal of Social Work.* Vol. 7, pp. 399-419.

Steinhilper, G., (1980) *An Experiment in Collaboration Between Police and Social Workers in Hanover (Federal Republic of Germany)* Paper presented to the International Conference, Strategies against Crime in Europe. Cranfield Institute of Technology, Cranfield, Bedford.

Van Maanen, J., (1978) 'People Processing: Strategies of Organisational Socialisation'. *Organisational Dynamics.* Summer, pp. 19-36.

Warham, J., (1977) *An Open Case. The Organisational Context of Social Work.* Routledge and Kegan Paul, London.

Weber, M., (1947) *The Theory of Social and Economic Organisation.* Free Press, New York.

Whyte, W.M., (1956) *The Organisation Man.* Simon and Schuster, New York.

Appendix 1

Interview schedule items

Organisational structure

Centralisation

Index of participation in decision making	Index of hierarchy of authority
1. How frequently do you participate in the decision concerning changes in the departmental budget?	1. There can be little action here until a supervisor approves a decision.
2. How frequently do you participate in the decision over the adoption of new services?	2. A person who wants to make his own decisions would be quickly discouraged here.
3. How frequently do you participate in the decision concerning the adoption of new policies?	3. Even small matters have to be referred to someone higher for a final answer.

For the index of participation in decision making, respondents were assigned numerical scores from 1 to 5, depending on whether they answered 'never', 'seldom', 'sometimes', 'often', or 'always' respectively to these items. For hierarchy of authority, responses could vary from 1 (definitely false) to 4 (definitely true).

Responses to job regulation were scored 1 (definitely true) to 4

Index of job regulation	Index of rule observation
1. A person can make his own decisions here without checking with anybody else.	1. The employees are constantly being checked for rule violations.
2. How things are done around here is left pretty much up to the person doing the work.	2. People feel as though they are constantly being watched to see that they obey all rules.
3. People here are allowed to do almost as they please.	

(definitely false), and with rule observation 4 (definitely true) to 1 (definitely false). Single questions were asked and scored concerning the presence of job descriptions and rules manuals, and the responses coded, 4 (complete), 3 (partly complete), 2 (just started) and 1 (non-existent).

Complexity

Complexity was a more difficult dimension to utilise. As our concern is with understanding the degree of professional and organisational complexity, a series of non-coded questions were asked and computed as follows:

Score

1. Length of training,
   1.1 absence of training beyond school and the absence of other professional training — 0
   1.2 absence of training in university/college level and absence of other professional training — 1
   1.3 presence of training to university/college level and absence of other professional training — 2
   1.4 advanced university training and absence of professional training — 3
   1.5 presence of training to university/college level and presence of other professional training — 4
   1.6 advanced university training and presence of professional training. — 5

2. Index of professional activity,
   2.1 one point for belonging to a professional association

178

2.2   one point for attending at least two-thirds of the previous six meetings of the professional association

2.3   one point for presenting a paper or holding office in a professional association.

3. Index of trade union activity,
   3.1   one point for belonging to a trade union
   3.2   one point for attending two-thirds of the previous six meetings
   3.3   one point for holding office

4. Index of occupational specialisation, one point allotted for each specialisation each respondent held.

Routineness of work

1. One thing people like around here is the variety of work
2. Most jobs have something new happening every day
3. There is something different to do every day.

Respondents replied 1 (definitely true) to 4 (definitely false) to each of the questions.

Appendix 2

Interview schedule items

Organisation and group culture

Challenge and responsibility

Index of job autonomy

1. How often (do) (did) you and your colleagues during the past year, make your own work decisions without checking with the next higher in the chain of command?

2. How often (do) (did) you and your colleagues, during the past year, receive direction from higher up?

3. How often (do) (did) you and your colleagues during the past year, have to refer even small matters to someone higher for a final answer?

Index of career fulfilment

1. How satisfied are you with your present job when you compare it to similar positions in other agencies or departments?

2. How satisfied are you with the progress you are making towards the goals which you set yourself in your present position?

3. How satisfied are you with your present job when you consider the expectations you had when you took the job?

4. How satisfied are you with your present job in the light of your career expectations?

5. How satisfied are you that you have been given enough authority to do your job well?

Responses to the index of job autonomy varied from 1 (always) to 5 (never) with the scoring reversed for question 1. Index of career fulfilment varied from 1 (very dissatisfied) to 4 (very satisfied).

Conflict

<table>
<tr><td colspan="2" align="center">Index of questioning
authority</td><td colspan="2" align="center">Index of interpersonal
aggression</td></tr>
<tr><td>1.</td><td>When people disagree with a decision they work to get it changed.</td><td>1.</td><td>Personal rivalries are fairly common in this place.</td></tr>
<tr><td>2.</td><td>People here are not likely to accept managerial ineptitude without complaint or protest.</td><td>2.</td><td>A lot of people in this place walk around with a chip on their shoulder.</td></tr>
<tr><td>3.</td><td>When people dislike policy, they let it be known in no uncertain terms.</td><td>3.</td><td>There always seem to be a lot of little quarrels going on here.</td></tr>
<tr><td></td><td></td><td>4.</td><td>People are always trying to win an argument.</td></tr>
<tr><td></td><td></td><td>5.</td><td>Many people here seem to brood a lot, act moodily and it is hard to make them out.</td></tr>
</table>

Response to both indices could vary from 1 (definitely false) to 4 (definitely true).

Warmth and support

The indices of job climate were computed on the basis of responses to the following items (managers were offered a separate item schedule containing questions relevant to their specific situation).

Index of job support or constraint (Staff/Supervisors)

1. The frequency with which your boss(es) involves you in setting goals is such that . . . . .

2. The knowledge, experience and ability of your boss(es) is such that . . . .

3. The extent to which your boss(es) give encouragement and support to your decisions and recommendations . . . .

4. The extent to which your boss(es) shows his confidence in your abilities is such that . . . .

5. Your boss(es) interpersonal skills (ability to listen, communicate, understand people) are such that . . . .

6. The extent to which your boss(es) is open to changing his mind is such that . . . .

7. The quality and accuracy of the information and communications you receive from your boss(es) is such that . . . .

8. The extent to which the goals and objectives set for your job are clear and unambiguous is such that . . . .

9. The enthusiasm and ability of your boss(es) to think of new ideas and creative solutions to problems is such that . . . .

Index of job support or constraint (managers)

1. The level of skill and knowledge of your subordinates is such that . . . .

2. The degree to which your subordinates need to be watched and supervised is such that . . . .

3. The level of work output shown by your subordinates is such that . . . .

4. The quality and accuracy of information and communications you receive from subordinates is such that . . . .

5. The interpersonal skills (ability to listen, communicate and understand people) of your subordinates, is such that . . . .

6. The amount of variety (opportunity to do a number of different things) is the jobs of your subordinates is such that . . . .

7. The degree to which your subordinates jobs provide chance to use knowledge, skills and abilities they value is such that . . . .

8. The degree to which your subordinates jobs are stimulating and interesting to them is such that . . . .

Response to both indices varied from 5 (great deal easier to do your job well) to 1 (great deal harder to do your job well).

Team performance rating index

Rank	Characteristics of team	How does this team compare with the departmental average?		
		Low	Average	High
( )	Quality of work			
( )	Volume of work produced . .			

Rank	Characteristics of team	How does this team compare with the departmental average?		
		Low	Average	High
( )	Order and system			
( )	Enthusiastic effort			
( )	Persistence against obstacles			
( )	Loyalty to the department . .			
( )	Harmony amongst team members			
( )	Freedom of members to act on own judgement			
( )	Support of the department in emergencies			
( )	Support of the team in emergencies			
( )	Co-operation with other teams			

Each respondent was given the following instructions on how to complete the team performance rating index.

Rating of team performance

Name of team being rated . . . .

Team supervised by . . . .

Instructions:

Please consider the entire work group or team named above. Rank and rate the performance of the unit as a whole, using the 11 items below.

1. Which of the 11 characteristics of team performance does the team do best? Which does it do poorest? Rank the different characteristics in order from 1 to 11 in the brackets to the left of the items. A

rank of (1) means that the team does better in this than in the other 10 performances. A rank of (2) means that it does next best in this performance. A rank of (11) means that the team does more poorly in this than in the other 10 performances.

2. Decide how this team stands in relations to the departmental average on each performance. Mark an X on the rating scale after each item to show how this unit compares with the departmental average. Scoring varied from 1 (low) to 4 (high).

Appendix 3

Further responses at social worker level

A. Social worker (metropolitan district — professionally qualified and three years in post)

What do you do in your job?
Well I think some of the tasks set, I would rather not tackle. This comes back to my disagreement with the Seebohm principle because I'd rather identify a particular client group or groups and deal with them than say other client groups. I don't want or don't feel competent with certain groups. Being in a generic social service department, I've got to take on tasks I don't want, which obviously means I've got some conflict with my occupation.

How do you feel about what you are doing?
My feelings about what I am doing are very much related to my relationship with my superior — my team leader. She is available for consultation over any problem at all. She does not carry any cases of her own. We are offered regular supervision which means the opportunity to talk about your cases and how you feel about them, what you felt your difficulties were and how they can be best ironed out.

What are you achieving by what you are doing?
I see my personal position as that of trying to gain some advancement in my office. My future position I see very much as raising the

level of awareness of social work and hopefully gain promotion as well.

What have you learned from what you are doing?
I have come to terms with the fact that I have to distance myself between me as a person and me as a professional social worker. One learns to detach oneself from the problem; this is where the distance comes in; to provide a caring relationship with people but not having the emotional closeness which one's personal relationships give.

B. Social worker (family service unit)

What do you do in your job?
We deal with a number of different clients and problems. I sometimes feel it is a little misleading to think of us as a Family Service Unit because I cannot really see the difference between what we do and the work of the generic teams.

How do you feel about what you are doing?
There is a lot of administrative work that seems to be growing. I suppose that the work at area office is connected with the work at central office. We are always being asked to provide them with statistics, not necessarily internally but for DHSS and other similar offices. We do not really know what they are for; we are just asked to supply the information.

What are you achieving by what you are doing?
Well, I would say taking an overall look, I think since re-organisation there has been an expansion of service amidst different types of services. But I suppose you tend to look at the negative side and get a bit depressed, rather than look at what has been achieved.

What have you learned from what you are doing?
I think there should be a better flow of communication between the social workers and the hierarchy. I think sometimes its done on a formal basis when really it does not mean anything. The management will come and talk to you about something but when they have finished talking, you're no wiser. So that causes more frustration than it being any help.

C. Social worker (county council — professionally qualified and two years in post)

What do you do in your job?
Administrative work . . . . . first of all it is very necessary and it can
be helpful to a social worker if it is done the way a social worker
wants it done. My experience is that it is sometimes done the way
administrative people want it done and that is not the same thing.

How do you feel about what you are doing?
My aim is to become far more community minded especially for
young offenders for whom I believe institutional care is not much
use.

What are you achieving by what you are doing?
Having decided to work on developing community facilities, I have
also decided to determine my own level of administration. I hope
this leaves me more time to do what I couldn't do before, although
I am not sure in the end that it will do so.

What have you learnt from what you are doing?
On the whole, I think the department is a bit top heavy. It tends to
be the wrong way round. In my experience you tend to have one
social worker for every ten administrative staff. I feel that because
of this we are doing nothing but statutory orders, we are doing
child care work at the expense of mental health activities.

Further responses at the senior social worker level

A. Senior social worker (county council — professionally qualified
with over three years in post)

What do you do in your job?
I like the job I do. I like being a senior social worker, because in a
sense it gives me more power to do things that I want to do; to
organise work in the area and to establish priorities to help social
workers.

How do you feel about what you are doing?
I think I am quite good as a teacher. I enjoy helping new social
workers in developing professional skills. I get a great amount of job
satisfaction out of that. I don't enjoy telling people what to do and
I don't enjoy shouting at people. Earlier, I had great hang-ups about
it, but not now. Sometimes, I cheat and ignore departmental policy
and take on a short-term case. I do this to improve myself in my
current job and I would really like to see myself doing this job for
another five or six years yet. There are a lot of pressures trying to

push me on — money, wife and the department itself.

What are you achieving by what you are doing?
Within my department, I am part of middle management. I feel
that a senior social worker's job, in this particular organisation is
important. It's a job where you have the opportunity to influence
things, to make decisions and yet you are only one step removed
from grass roots social work. As a result you see what is going on.
You wield a great deal of power in the department simply because
you are near to where it is being practised, so you have a lot of
information about practise that people higher in the bureaucracy
do not have. I am probably seen as a radical, but in general, I think
that my department is a passive reactionary sort of organisation,
which probably makes me quite moderate.

What have you learnt from what you are doing?
Social service organisations are hierarchical as they are part of
local government bureaucracy. Decisions are made by people who
are most removed from the problems. However, I also think there
are some good things. That social services are organised on a generic
basis, rationalises the procedure for intervention into social situations. It is based on the family rather than individuals and I think
this is important. I think it is the most important supportive institution in society, but it can get better. The real problem is that we
do not have enough skilled managers in social work, and industry in
this sense is way ahead of us. We need to develop skills in dealing
with people, in being able to delegate responsibility, to make
decisions and to be able to liaise with other organisations.

B. Senior social worker (metropolitan district — professionally qualified with five years senior social work experience)

What do you do in your job?
First, I do not have any clients. Second, I allocate work and supervise social workers. I also have some administrative tasks.

How do you feel about what you are doing?
I find a lot of the clerical work unnecessary. Sometimes I get bored
with the job and other times I find it stimulating. Each individual
social worker presents tasks to me which I don't see as a problem
in doing my job. I suppose the major problem is in coping with
myself . . . occasional disenchantment with social work.

What are you achieving by what you are doing?
I suppose I see my main strengths as being able to facilitate an

190

atmosphere within this particular office which is good relationships and which means therefore that energy is not wasted with in-fighting within the office. In addition, I suppose another strength that I would see would be in terms of developing systems of work. I would hope I am achieving more efficient ways of coping, being able to hold back cases and not to drop them on people because I don't want them on my desk.

What have you learnt from what you are doing?
It was hard at first to say 'No', laying down the departmental line when necessary. I have also learnt to shut up and not to brow beat people into them doing what I want them to. I also like the idea of being rapidly promoted and hence change. At first, there were many positions to apply for, but now there are not so many. However, people are still trying to change their jobs in order to get as much experience as possible so that they can be promoted. I think I have learnt to stay put and develop the social work side of the job instead of just my career.

C. Senior social worker (metropolitan district — professionally quali-fied with five years experience at senior level)

What do you do in your job?
I see the purpose of the job to sift out the priorities of referrals that come through to the department and attempt to allocate them to social workers in my team appropriately, according to the case load they already have and expertise and their personal develop-ment as social workers . . . . During my working day, apart from allocating work and discussing cases with social workers informally, I have the responsibility of calling team members to further discuss decisions made by top management and passing down information quickly to the team so that they can have knowledge of decisions made at a higher level.

How do you feel about what you are doing?
As far as administration is concerned . . . it appears to be very time-consuming working out levels of service and getting the figures to balance at the end of the month. It seems very bureaucratic and frustrating . . . do we give priority to the bureaucracy or do we give priority to the job we are doing on the social work side.

What are you achieving by what you are doing?
I see my role as providing as good a service as possible through the social workers to the clients . . . by guiding the social workers and to indicate to them through our meetings, the policy decisions and

remind them of the financial restrictions that we have. It is an important thing to allocate the work to the right person to provide a better service through people — relationships.

What have you learnt from what you are doing?
My feelings about the past is that we were feeding clients with money and resources too readily, too early and I think during the last five years we have as an office, encouraged clients to more self-help, to look at their own problems. Hence, they can see why they are in the situation they are, and to develop the client's own self-help in that way through practical communication within the families, through more intensive casework.

Further responses from the managerial group

A. Area officer (metropolitan district — qualified with eight years social work experience)

What do you do in your job?
The tasks that I set are mainly to do with the incoming work of the department for the staff; my own role is being able to decide where the work should go. I have two good seniors to whom I can delegate. I try and balance the needs of the area in relation to the ability of the staff. For example, my deputy, who is very able, very aggressive, very professional, which at times needs watering down into my own sort of welfare orientation and client interaction. I feel it necessary to play a sort of father figure to get the clients something and work on the department's problems.

How do you feel about what you are doing?
I see myself as being a very average area officer. It's too easy to sit behind a big desk keeping the clients at bay and thinking you have a God given right to go round administering policies. I don't do any of those things. I do not even have a big desk. I do not think it is my job to go round administering policy. In fact, I think I spend most of my time trying to change policy rather than administering it. I think it is my job to reflect the views of clients, staff and my perception of the area's needs, in that order.

What are you achieving by what you are doing?
Well, as an area officer, I am in a funny situation. I have to achieve good working relationships and establish policies that are workable in practise. This puts me in the situation that I have to deal with complaints from staff and clients. Some clients feel agrieved at

the department and think it necessary to go to a higher authority to complain or even chastise members of our staff. I don't mind this, because sometimes, it is our staff that have missed the point but never maliciously I think. Occasionally, we have a specific complaint of social workers attitudes towards specific clients. All that goes to show that if you want social workers but have not got enough of them, you're bound to get sometimes the wrong social workers with the wrong clients. In addition, we have disagreements with members of staff; I suppose really, my staff see me as a 'gripes Ombudsman' both ways, about clients and about themselves. It is not just the clients who have their way through to me but my own staff about clients and each other.

What have you learnt from what you are doing?
The think that I have learnt most as being problematic is the perceived discrepancy between the problem the client has and the problem society will accept. Two different problems, but in reality measures have to be made available through committee to the department to meet these problems. I can tell you right now, counsellors are a real problem. They are not too keen on battered wives and they certainly dislike psychiatrically disturbed patients, who are often described as scroungers. Problems we have to cope with are that neither legislation nor politicians accept certain difficulties as problems. So what I have learnt is that you have to manipulate the system; identify clients needs and try and get the system to accept those needs.

B. Assistant director (metropolitan district — professionally qualified with many years experience in social work)

What do you do in your job?
First, the responsibility to run a large area team; secondly to act as a member of the departmental management team and thirdly to act as an adviser to the Department on matters relating to children. My job is to pass information down to my subordinate managers and in turn they bring problems to me to present to the D.M.T. (Department Management Team). Once a month there is a complete Area meeting with all staff of all descriptions so that this is used as a balancing exercise to ensure that nothing is missed coming down or going up.

How do you feel about what you are doing?
I feel that we have got a system of management which goes from top to bottom and from the bottom to the top through its normal processes so that everybody is able to contribute to the situation.

What are you achieving by what you are doing?
The object of this is to achieve a unified and good service to the client in the community.

What have you learnt from what you are doing?
I have learnt that we are local government officers first, and social workers second. So therefore, there are constraints to begin with that nobody can act outside the law and nobody can act outside their policy. The policy comes down from Committee and although we cannot influence policy at the various meetings they still take place as a matter of course.

Index

Managers, SSD (cont.)
training 166-8, 169; views of directors' seminar 5-6
March, J.G. and Simon, A.A. 77
Marran, B. and Buchanan, B. 134, 135
Maud Report 51
Meltzer, L. and Slater, J. 26
Morgan, J.B. on Police/Social Services Juvenile Bureau in Exeter 138-9
Morris, P. 133, 134
Mott, J. 147
Mumford, E. 110

National Health Service 39, 43; reformed to suit local government boundaries 51
National Society for the Prevention of Cruelty to Children 133-4
Newman, A.D. and Rowbottom, R.W. 43n

Organisations 2; complexity of relationships in 27-35; culture of, see separate entry; divisional structure 31; functional structure 30-1; hierarchical structure 27, 29; influence on individuals 2-3; integrating the person with 151-2; macro-micro development model 121; matrix structure 31-3; organisational iceberg 152, 153; problems of managerial control 27, 30, 33-5; problems of reorganisation 25; professional v. organisational values 35-9; question of competent supervision 34-5; question of size 26-7, 39; reasons for analysing structure of 24-6

Parsloe, P. and Stephenson, O. 108, 139, 148; on consultants 139-40
Payne, Roy: and Phesey, D.C. 55n; his Organisational Supports or Constraints Questionnaire 55
Plan of book 7-8, 119-20
Police: Police/Social Services Juvenile Bureau 138-9; relations with social services 105-6
Post Office: role culture in 18
Pritchard, R.D. and Karasick, B.W. 110
Professionalism 35-6; key factors determining 35
Pugh et al. 29

Rowbottom, R.W. 18, 31, 44, 47; and Hey, A.M. 46; et al. 43, 44n, 45, 46
Russell, Peter 85

Salmon Report 51
Schumacher, E.F. 26
Seebohm Report 7, 26, 42, 51, 52, 92
Semi-professions 37, 38
Smith, G. 147
Social Service Departments (SSDs): achieving planned integration 148-9, 150; areas of contradiction 111-114, 115; arguments for centralisation 125-6; arguments for decentralisation 126-7; career development 110-11, 115; centralisation/decentralisation arguments 124-8, 149; complexity of relationships in 27-35, 72; cultural norms and values in 105-10; example of recruiting practice 3-5;

Social Service Departments (SSDs) (cont.)

factors influencing design of 146, 147; gamesmanship in 113, 114, 115; 'gatekeepers' 108, 109, 110, 114, 115; improving individuals' motivation 131; improving long-term planning 129-30; improving managerial control 130; internal consultants in 32, 139-44, 149-50; job climate indices 74, 76, 77, 79; learning processes 111-14, 115; management information system (MIS) improvement 128-31, 149; management problems in 152-68; manager level perceptions of culture 73, 75; mix of cultures in 105-14; need for a language for 6; opposition to consultants in metropolitan district SSD 141-2; organisational identity in 79-82; outside consultants 144-5; problem solving steps for managers 157-68; professional satellite team concept 131-9, 148, 149; professional v. organisational values 35-9; question of further reform 145-9, 150; question of importance of hierarchy of authority 59-62; question of importance of participation in decision making 59, 60; question of re-designing 123-4; question of size 26-7, 39, 65-6; reducing conflict in 131; relation of structural properties of 62-5; relations with local councillors 155-6; relations with police 105-6, 138-9; relationship between complexity of relations and organisation culture 72; relationship between formality of procedure and organisation culture 70; relationship between hierarchy of authority and organisation culture 69; relationship between structure and culture 68-71, 72; residential officers' attitudes to the job 94-8, 103, 104; senior social workers' attitudes to the job 90-4, 103, 104, 108; social work managers' attitudes to the job 98-103, 104, 105; social workers' attitudes to the job 87-90, 103, 104, 107; staff characteristics compared with academics and engineers 80-2, 106-7; stages of research into culture in 54-7; studies of organisation culture in 53 *et seq.*; studies of social workers at work 133-4; study of culture at group level in 71, 73-83; study of culture at individual level in 84-105; study of culture at organisation level in 67-71, 82, 83; study of organisation structure in nine SSDs 57-9, 62, 67; study of task processes 86; supervision in 107-8, 109; supervisor level perceptions of culture 75, 77; task analysis at individual level 84-6; task/role culture conflict in rural county SSD 143-4; views of directors' seminar 5-6